I0410716

Contents

Front cover photo: Holm Oak (*Quercus ilex*), by Ian Parsons

Back cover photo: The author, by Jo Parsons

Introduction

"Friendship is a sheltering tree."

Samuel Taylor Coleridge

Wherever you are in the world reading this, the odds are that if you look around you, or out of your window, you will be able to see at least one tree. Trees are everywhere, we plant them, we use them, we play in them, we draw them, we appreciate them, we fell them, we burn them, we exploit them. We do lots to trees, but do we actually know that much about them.

A Miscellany of Trees is a book packed full of facts about these wonderful entities that are all around us. Facts that will make you think a bit more about what we can consider as everyday objects, facts that will make you smile, even facts that might make you angry.

Trees are wonderful things and for the fan of miscellany they are an incredible resource! So read on and enjoy and discover not only what are the oldest and tallest trees in the world, but also which trees can survive nuclear blasts and which ones are banned from public transport...

To Begin...

"I never saw a discontented tree."

John Muir

Let's start with a simple question shall we. What is a tree? Surely one of the more simple questions there is. But try answering it though. You see, that's the tricky part. If you've just tried to answer it and have come up with adjectives such as Tall and Big then I am afraid you are wrong. Maybe you thought a bit harder and used words such as wood or woody and stem, or perhaps you even used the clever sounding Lignin. Guess what? Wrong.

The problem is that trees aren't a homogenous bunch, whilst some are closely related to one another, others are very, very unrelated indeed. As a result, there is no biological definition of what makes a tree a tree. Fish are fish, mammals are mammals, trees are... well that's just it. There is, if you like, no such thing as a tree.

Trees are plants and belong to all parts of this highly varied Kingdom. They are so spread out across it, that a Christmas tree is as closely related to an Oak tree, as we are to a flat fish.

Therefore the answer to that simple question goes along the lines of the following: A tree is a colloquial term applied to a diverse selection of often unrelated plants that have evolved similar characteristics in terms of their general appearance. A bit dull really.

Of course, whilst trees might not exist in the true scientific sense, they very much exist in our everyday world. A good job really, considering I have just written this book about them! We love trees, they are all around us and many of us get very passionate when we hear of threats towards them. Trees form a vital part of our planets diversity, without them many other species of plant, animal and fungi simply would not exist. We probably wouldn't exist.

We evolved in trees. The highly complex structure of their branches led to us developing long fore limbs and dextrous hands. As these features evolved, so too did our intelligence, enabling us to use these limbs effectively and successfully in the multi layered world of a woodland. There were, of course, other creatures in this world, but by a quirk of fate it was our ancestors that evolved into the dominant species of planet Earth. If parallel universes do exist, there may well be one in which a form of Squirrel drives to work on a Monday morning, sitting in traffic that crawls slowly along, past the city park, from within which, a small ape like creature looks on from high up in the trees.

Vital Statistics

"When you have seen one ant, one bird, one tree, you have not seen them all."

E.O. Wilson

What is the oldest tree in the world, what is the tallest, what is the biggest etc etc etc. This chapter looks at the answers to these questions, as well as many more as it explores the world of tree statistics.

First of all though, just how many trees are there? It has been estimated that there could be around 60,000 species of tree in the world. However, the truth is, no one really knows just how many are out there.

So then, what is the oldest tree in the world? This is probably one of the commonest questions I have been asked. However, it is not always straightforward to answer, as it comes down to the 'What is a tree?' question again... On top of that, the age of trees is often greatly overestimated, with many Yew trees in Britain, for example, having been given fantastic ages based on pure guesswork. On a basic level the following are the oldest trees in the world that have an actual verified age.

SPECIES	AGE (as of 2016)
Great Basin Bristlecone Pine	5,065
Great Basin Bristlecone Pine	4,848
Great Basin Bristlecone Pine	4,845
Patagonian Cypress	3,645
Giant Sequoia	3,267
Giant Sequoia	3,221
Giant Sequoia	3,201
Giant Sequoia	3,076
Giant Sequoia	3,034
Western Juniper	2,676

But, and it is a big but, recent advancements in DNA science has discovered that some 'trees' are only the current active stem or stems of a bigger clonal root system. The following clonal trees have been aged by radiocarbon dating. At the time of writing, late 2016, these are the top four oldest trees, but as further studies are undertaken this list is likely to change.

SPECIES	AGE	NAME
Quaking Aspen	80,000	Pando
Palmer Oak	13,000	Jurupa Oak
Norway Spruce	9,550	Old Tjikko
Norway Spruce	9,500	Old Rasmus

This potentially makes Pando not only the oldest tree in the world, but also the oldest currently living organism on the planet. It is also the heaviest, weighing in at an estimated 6,000 tonnes.

In the 1960s, Archaeologists working in the Middle East discovered a pottery vase that contained the seeds of the Date Palm. Radio carbon dating put their age at 2,000 years old. After then being stored for forty more years, three of the seeds were planted, one of which germinated, making it the oldest known viable seed ever. The young tree is still growing and is now over two metres tall.

The Fortingall Yew of Perthshire in Scotland, is probably Britain's oldest tree. Yew trees are virtually impossible to age accurately, as their heartwood rots away leaving no annual rings to count. Estimates vary wildly, but it is now widely believed to be about 2,000 years old.

When experts studied the genetics of a group of Small-leaved Lime trees growing at Westonbirt arboretum in Gloucestershire, they discovered that they were actually all part of the same tree. It is believed that the tree has been repeatedly coppiced over hundreds of years, and the ring of stools today is actually the edge of the original tree with the centre now rotted away. The tree is believed to be over 2,000 years old.

The Bowthorpe Oak in Lincolnshire is believed to be Britain's oldest Oak tree at over 1,000 years old.

The Tortworth Chestnut, just off the M5 motorway in Gloucestershire, is a large Sweet Chestnut that, thanks to a number of branches that have rooted into the ground, looks like a group of trees rather than just one. No one knows its age, but it is mentioned in a document dating from 1166 as being a notable landmark called the Great Chestnut of Tortworth and that was over 850 years ago.

The Hundred Horse Chestnut of Sicily is the largest and (probably) the oldest Sweet Chestnut in the world, with an estimated age of 4,000 years. It gets the potentially confusing name from the story that the visiting Queen of Aragon and her court (a total of 100 mounted people,) were caught in a sudden rain storm, forcing them to all take shelter under the tree. The age of the tree is even more incredible given its location; it sits on the slopes of Mount Etna (a very active volcano whose latest eruption was in December 2015) and is just five miles from the volcano's crater.

The Kongeegen or King Oak of Denmark, is widely believed to be the oldest Oak in Europe, having an estimated age of 1500 – 2000 years.

Baikushev's Pine in Bulgaria is a Bosnian Pine that is believed to be the oldest Pine tree in Europe with an estimated age of 1300 years.

The Olive Tree of Vouves on the Greek island of Crete, is believed to be the oldest Olive Tree in the world. Ring analysis dates it to be at least 2,000 years old, but with the centre of the tree hollowed out, it is even older than that, with some estimates putting it at approximately 4,000 years old. It still produces Olives.

The oldest living tree in New York is a Field Elm growing in Manhattan, known locally as the Hangman's Elm it is 337 years old.

The oldest living cultivated fruit tree in America, is a European Common Pear that was planted by the governor of the newly created Massachusetts Bay Colony in the 1630s.

As for the question, what is the tallest tree in the world? That is a bit easier, although the reason that these are the current tallest has all to do with ourselves and is dealt with in a later chapter.

Top 10 Tallest Trees Still Living

Species	Height (m)	Location
Coast Redwood	118.6	USA
Mountain Ash Eucalyptus	99.8	Australia
Douglas Fir	99.7	USA
Sitka Spruce	96.7	USA
Giant Sequoia	95.8	USA
Manna Gum	91	Australia
Southern Blue Gum	90.7	Australia
Noble Fir	89.9	USA
Klinki Pine	89	New Guinea
Alpine Ash Eucalyptus	88.7	Australia

However, the tallest tree in the world is not the highest. The Fir Tree *Abies squamata* is the highest tree in the world. It grows on the Tibetan plateau at 4,400 metres above sea level.

The tallest known pine tree in the world is a Western Yellow Pine growing in Oregon in America. In 2011 it measured 81.77m tall.

The tallest tree in Britain is a Douglas Fir in Scotland. When last measured it was 66.4 metres tall and, at around 150 years of age, it is still a youngster with plenty of growth to come.

The tallest non conifer tree in the world and therefore the world's tallest flowering plant, is the Mountain Ash Eucalyptus, measuring around 100m tall.

At the complete opposite end of all this tallness, is the Mountain Willow, native to parts of Scotland, it rarely gets above 50cms in height. But this is a giant when compared to the Arctic Willow, which is typically only 15cms high. Don't let the lack of height make you think that they are short in terms of age though; one Arctic Willow was 236 years old.

But what about the biggest tree in the world? There are two ways of measuring 'big', the first is by volume:

Top 10 Largest Trees by Volume Still Living

Species	Volume	Location
Giant Sequoia	1487m³	USA
Coast Redwood	1084m³	USA
Montezuma Cypress	750m³	Mexico
Kauri	516m³	New Zealand
Western Redcedar	500m³	USA
Mountain Ash Eucalyptus	391m³	Australia
Tasmanian Blue Gum	368m³	Australia
Douglas Fir	349m³	USA
Sitka Spruce	337m³	USA
Eucalyptus obliqua	337m³	Australia

The second is by diameter at breast height, which is commonly referred to as dbh. This measurement is taken at 1.3 metres from the ground using a specially graduated tape that goes around the tree's circumference but is actually measuring the diameter.

Top 10 Largest Trees by Diameter Still Living

Species	Diameter (m)	Location
Montezuma Cypress	11.62	Mexico
Baobab	10.64	South Africa
Giant Sequoia	8.85	USA
Za	8.85	Madagascar
Chinese Camphor Tree	8.23	Japan
Coast Redwood	7.90	USA
Eucalyptus oblique	6.72	Australia
Mountain Ash Eucalyptus	6.52	Australia
Western Redcedar	5.94	USA
Alpine Ash Eucalyptus	5.82	Australia

Therefore the above Montezuma Cypress, also known as the Tree of Tule, in Mexico, is the world's fattest tree, having the largest diameter of any plant, anywhere in the world. The girth, or circumference, of this huge tree actually measures over 42 metres. It is known locally as Ahuehuete, which means old man of the water in the local language. It is believed to have been planted 1400 years ago by a follower of the Aztec God of Wind.

Trees can also be very large in terms of how far their canopy spreads, as proved by a Oriental Plane tree growing in Corsham, Wiltshire. It is officially the UK's tree with the largest spread of branches. Planted by the famous landscape designer Capability Brown in 1760, the branch spread of this single tree covers roughly the size of a football pitch.

The Dodda Aladha Mara is a Banyan Tree growing in India. It covers three acres in size and actually looks like a grove of separate trees. However, the separate 'stems' have all rooted from branches from the original stem that has subsequently died and rotted away.

The brilliantly named Wonderboom Tree of South Africa, is a large fig tree whose original trunk is over a thousand years old. Over time, branches from the original trunk touched the ground, rooted, and then sent up trunks of their own, forming a ring around the original stem. In turn, branches from these new stems did exactly the same. There are now three rings of stems surrounding the original one, and in total, the Fig covers an area of over 50 square metres.

And if you think that is nuts... The world's biggest Cashew tree can be found growing in Brazil, the canopy of the tree is absolutely huge, covering over one hectare of land. It produces around 60,000 Cashew nuts every year.

Talking of seeds, which of course is what nuts are, *Lodoicea maldivica*, also known as the Sea Coconut, is a species of Palm that grows in the Maldives in the Indian Ocean. The fruits of the species are known as Coco de Mer and are the heaviest fruit anywhere in the plant kingdom, with one recorded weighing 42kgs! Unsurprisingly, the seed within the fruit is the heaviest seed in the world, weighing in at over 17kgs. The flowers that produce these fruits are also the largest flowers of any palm.

The largest tree borne fruit in the world belongs to the Jackfruit Tree of India. It can measure up to 90cms in length with a diameter of 50cms. An individual tree can produce up to 200 of these giant fruits every year. The fruits are edible and are widely used in all sorts of cuisine, as well as being used to make an alcoholic drink.

The South American tree *Berthollettia excels* is the tree that gives us the Brazil nut. Up to two dozen Brazil nuts are tightly packed into the trees fruit, which itself is encased in a hard shell up to 15cms in diameter and weighing in at up to 2kgs. It resembles a small bowling ball, and bowling balls dropping from heights of up to 50 metres are going to cause damage. Every year, vehicles and houses are damaged and people injured and even killed by Brazil nuts as they fall to earth, packed into their solid casing.

If you thought bowling balls were bad, the Cannonball Tree of South America produces even bigger fruits than that of the Brazil nut tree. These spherical fruits of up to 25cms in diameter do indeed resemble Cannonballs.

Trees aren't just what we can see above the ground, their roots are just as impressive, with the South African Fig having roots that measure almost 120 metres in length.

These roots find water for the tree and they do so in prodigious amounts. The trees take the water from the soil, using their roots, and draw it up the tree before they discharge it back into the air via their leaves. This process is called Transpiration. A large healthy tree can transpire 800 pints of water a day.

We might not think of trees being that fast, but the White Mulberry tree is the fastest plant in the world. Well, the stamens of it are at least. When the pollen is released, the stamens catapult forward at about 350 miles per hour. This is the fastest recorded movement in the entire plant kingdom.

Possibly the rarest tree in Britain and one of the rarest in the world, is the Catacol Whitebeam. It is only found growing on the Isle of Arran, off the west coast of Scotland. There are just two known examples of it.

The world's most photographed tree is believed to be a Monterey Cypress that has been given the name of the Lone

Cypress. It grows on a cliff top overlooking the sea near the city of Monterey in California.

Since 2011 there has been an annual European Tree of the Year award. The winners are as follows:

Year	Species	Location
2011	Small-leaved Lime	Romania
2012	Small-leaved Lime	Hungary
2013	London Plane	Hungary
2014	Field Elm	Bulgaria
2015	Pedunculate Oak	Estonia
2016	Downy Oak	Hungary

Britain's tree of the year in 2015, as voted for by the public, was the Cubbington Pear growing in Warwickshire. It is due to be cut down to make way for the HS2 rail project.

The wood of the Balsa tree weighs 44kgs per cubic metre, the wood of the Black Ironwood weighs 1490kgs per cubic metre. That makes the Black Ironwood almost 34 times heavier than the Balsa per cubic metre of timber. This again highlights the differences between the many species of what we call trees.

Finally, to give you something to think about, it is estimated that over 25% of medicines that we use originate from rainforests, yet only 1% of rainforest plants have been so far studied for their medicinal properties.

The Name Game

"The tree of knowledge is not the tree of life."

Lord Byron

We humans love to give everything a name. These names can sometimes be insightful and at other times they can be a bit daft. More often than not though, they are just plain wrong.

Acer means sharp, relating to the historical use of maple poles by the Romans and the Greeks, who used them to make spear shafts.

Horse chestnuts could have got their name from a series of errors, firstly they are not chestnuts and secondly it was thought that if these non chestnuts were fed to horses it would cure them of chest complaints. In fact they are actually poisonous to horses.

The Tree of Heaven is a species originally from China, its English name sounds majestic, but its original Chinese one doesn't. It means foul smelling tree, which is somewhat slightly less majestic.

The Monkey Puzzle, or Monkey's despair as it is called in French, is said to have obtained this appellation from the remarks of Victorian lawyer Charles Austin who, on first seeing an example, remarked "It would puzzle a monkey to climb that".

The Handkerchief Tree gets its English name from the wonderful large flowers that it produces. The large, white petals reminded the children of the colonial staff in India, of people waving handkerchiefs to say goodbye, as they sailed from Britain to the colonies.

The Handkerchief Tree's Latin name is *Davidia*, it was named after the French missionary and botanist who first discovered it, Armand David. David also discovered the Pere David's Deer and was the first westerner to discover the Giant Panda.

The Ginkgo tree, which is sometimes called the living fossil, owes its name to a spelling mistake made by a western naturalist over 300 years ago. The name should have been translated as Ginkjo.

The Tulip Tree's Latin genus name, Liriodendron, actually means Lily Tree.

The Scots Pine is poorly named, it is not Scottish. It's native range extends from western Europe through to eastern Siberia. It can be found in the far north, extending into the Arctic Circle, and as far south as Asiatic Turkey. It does grow in Scotland though.

Likewise the English Oak, or as it should be called, Pedunculate Oak, is also found throughout Europe and well into Asia and therefore shouldn't really be called English. To confuse things even further, it is also known as French Oak...

The Douglas Fir has a problem with it's name. Firstly, it is not actually a Fir, but a Pseudotsuga (which means false hemlock), secondly, the name Douglas refers to Scottish botanist David Douglas who didn't discover the tree himself, but did introduce it in to cultivation. The discoverer of the tree was another botanist called Archibald Menzies, and it is his surname that forms the Latin name for the species, *Pseudotsuga menziesii*. In life the two men were great rivals who didn't see eye to eye, so it seems appropriate that the names for the tree appear to take sides too.

Unusually in the world of scientific names, two very different genera share the same genus name. Cryptomeria is the genus of the Japanese Cedar tree, it is also a genus of moths that are, of course, completely unrelated to the trees.

The Red Acacia of Africa has the unfortunate common name of Shittah tree. In religion, the Ark of the Covenant was said to have been made from the wood of the Shittah tree.

The Brazilwood tree of South America is famous for two things. Firstly, the beautiful timber of this species is highly sought after for making high value bows for stringed instruments, any other timber is considered inferior for the purpose. Secondly, it has a country named after it, not many trees can say that. The original name for Brazil was Terra do Brazil, which is Portuguese meaning Land of the Brazilwood tree, eventually the country's name was shortened to just plain old Brazil.

The Bastard Poon tree has an issue with names, not only is its common name unfortunate, but so is the scientific one, *Sterculia foetida*, which literally means stinking dung. But then it does stink, really stink, supposedly smelling like an open sewer. Not one for the garden then.

The Queensland Maple tree of Australia, is a tree that produces timber that resembles mahogany. It is actually part of the Citrus family and is much more closely related to the Lemon than it is to any Maple.

A Whitebeam species, that is found nowhere else in the world other than in North Devon, is called the No Parking Whitebeam. This strange name is a result of the first tree to be noticed by biologists in the 1930s, having a wooden No Parking sign nailed to it. The Latin name for the tree is *Sorbus admonitor* – admonitor refers to the tree and it's sign admonishing those motorists that dared to park underneath it.

The timber produced by *Eucalyptus regnans* is called Tasmanian Oak if the tree is grown in Tasmania, but it is known as Victorian Ash if grown in the state of Victoria. The tree is obviously a Eucalyptus and not either an Oak or an Ash. To confuse things even further, the common name for the tree is the Mountain Ash, which is, of course, another name for the Rowan tree which is in the Whitebeam family.

Conifers are routinely referred to as Evergreens, but there are some species of conifer that are actually deciduous. The Larch family is probably the best known example, making the Larch a deciduous evergreen...

Of Trees and Men

"A tree's a tree. How many more do you need to look at?"
Ronald Reagan

In this chapter we look at our relationship with trees, as well as the less than savoury things that we sometimes use them for. Unfortunately, as the ex-American president's quote demonstrates, trees aren't always appreciated in the manner that they deserve.

The tallest tree in the world at the moment is the Coast Redwood. This is only because man hasn't cut it down yet. That may sound flippant, but both Douglas Fir and Mountain Ash Eucalyptus have produced taller examples, but, because we value their timber more than the Coast Redwoods, they were cut down before we actually valued them for what they actually were. The practice of felling old growth forest areas full of huge majestic trees still continues. If left alone, the current tallest Douglas Firs and Mountain Ash Eucalyptus will overtake the Coast Redwood within 100 years.

The Coast Redwoods may be the current tallest trees in the world, but these magnificent plants are just the remnants of what was once an amazing Redwood forest. It is estimated that

95% of the old growth Redwood forests have been cleared by man since 1850.

To stop an American timber company from cutting down a thousand year old Coast Redwood tree, Julia Butterfly Hill climbed into the tree in December 1997 and stayed there for 738 days. It was only after all that time, as well as lots of public support, that the timber company finally agreed to spare the giant tree.

Trees have often been used for political purposes, sometimes benignly as in these examples.

The Tolpuddle Martyrs formed their trade union under a Sycamore tree growing in their Dorset village. They were punished for this 'outrage' by being deported to Australia.

In Slovakia, a Small-leaved Lime tree plays host to a national meeting of the country's politicians every year. The tree is believed to be over 700 years old and the meeting takes place under its branches.

Some trees become the subject of political debate such as the Lesser Whitebeam. The tree is a rare endemic to south Wales, found nowhere else in the world. It is also unusual in that an intervention in the House of Commons probably saved the tree from extinction. In 1947 the area where the tree can be found was being used by the British Army for mortar practice, unsurprisingly, this was having a rather detrimental effect on the wellbeing of the trees. The MP for the area raised the issue in parliament and persuaded the War Secretary to pull the army out of the area.

Whilst some trees need political decisions... The fruit of the Durian tree is one of those things that you either love or hate. The edible and highly nutritious fruit of South East Asia has been described by some as having a beautiful sweet smelling fragrance. Others, however, describe it as smelling revoltingly like raw sewage. To avoid potential arguments between commuters, the Malaysian parliament banned Durian fruit on public transport in the country.

Particular trees can become symbolic in terms of political causes. This happened in the American war of independence, when Elm trees became particularly linked with the American cause. In 1765 the first meetings of the colonists, who were resisting the imposition of British taxes, took place in front of an American White Elm in Boston. The British in 1775 deliberately felled the tree, knowing it to be symbolic to the growing revolution. In response, the Elm tree symbol was widely used in the flags of the American forces as they fought the British. The wooden yoke of the Liberty Bell was made from another Elm species, the Slippery Elm.

Usually, when individual trees become associated with particular causes, the trees can often come off worse. This can happen when trees are planted to celebrate a cause... In the year 2000, an aerial survey of a German forest revealed a group of European Larch trees planted in the shape of the Swastika, their brighter green foliage causing the symbol to stand out amidst the darker spruces. It is thought that the trees had been planted in 1938 by a Nazi party official. The trees were subsequently felled to remove the symbol.

...Or, when the tree has been planted by a famous figure. The playwright William Shakespeare planted a Mulberry Tree in his garden in Stratford in England. The tree became very famous and for a while was the must see tree in the country. In the 1750s however, it was cut down by the new owner of the property who had become fed up with the constant demands for access to it by sightseers. The owner was a reverend who obviously wasn't very beneficent.

More problems occur for trees that weren't necessary planted by anyone in particular, but have become associated, through no fault of their own, with a political cause. This was the case when the last emperor of the Chinese Ming dynasty hung himself in a Pagoda Tree in 1644. The tree became a famous national landmark, earning itself the name of Zuihuai (Guilty Pagoda Tree). It was uprooted and killed during the Cultural Revolution between 1966 and 1976.

The Three Branched Pine in Catalonia, Spain, is considered to be a symbol of Catalan nationalism, despite being dead for more than 100 years. In 2014, someone used a chainsaw to fell one of the three stems. It was subsequently reattached at a cost of €35,000.

The Pine of Tsar Dusan, was a Bosnian Pine tree that had been planted in Kosovo by Emperor Dusan, who was the then King of Serbia, in 1336. In the aftermath of the Kosovan war in 1999, the almost 700 year old tree was cut down and burnt as a symbol of the modern Serbian regime.

The Tree of Knowledge was a Ghost Gum Eucalyptus growing in Queensland in Australia. In 1892 a meeting was held under the tree in which the Australian Labour Party was formed. The tree became a symbol of the Australian political movement before, in 2006, someone deliberately killed it using a pesticide.

One Tree Hill in New Zealand is an important memorial site for both Maori and western settlers. It has also been a symbol of the conflict between the two peoples. When Auckland was founded at the foot of the hill, a large single tree grew on the summit, this tree was considered sacred by the Maori. In 1852 a settler deliberately cut the tree down. A number of trees were planted in 1870 to replace it, but unfortunately, the only ones to grow were two non native Maritime Pines. Both of the trees became symbolic of how settlers were imposing themselves on Maori culture. In 1960 one of these was felled, leaving just one tree on One Tree Hill again. In the year 2000, this tree was badly damaged and had to be felled, after Maori activists attacked it. After much political argument it was finally agreed in October 2015 that a grove of native trees will be planted at the summit in 2016 as a symbol of reconciliation.

One tree that has been a potent symbol of a political cause is the Tree of Guernica, the fifth incarnation of which survives today. The Tree of Guernica is a symbol of Basque nationalism in the town of Guernica in Northern Spain. There have been five 'Trees of Guernica' since the 14th century, the third one was planted in 1858 and survived the carpet bombing of the Luftwaffe in the Spanish civil war, eventually succumbing to fungus attack in 2004. The fourth one, planted before the demise of the third, only lasted 29 years before a fifth was planted in March 2015.

Some trees have no association with a cause other than in an individual's head, they too can suffer. A rare mutation in a Sitka Spruce growing in British Columbia, Canada, caused its foliage to be completely golden in colour. The tree, known as The Golden Spruce, was cut down illegally in 1997 by Grant Hadwin, apparently as a protest against logging companies. Before he could be tried, Grant Hadwin disappeared and has never been seen since.

Trees are also exploited in warfare, sometimes without harming the tree. It was a tradition in Roman times, before a battle, that the soldiers all received a breakfast of porridge made from Sweet Chestnuts.

In World War 1, the unrelated Horse Chestnuts had their conkers used in the process for producing cordite for ammunition manufacture in Britain.

Trees have long been harvested for their products to be used in warfare. The battle of Agincourt in 1415, where the English defeated the French, is famous for the use of the 'English' Longbow. These longbows were made from Yew wood, but the British climate is not ideal for growing long, knot free yew timber and therefore the majority of the Yew timber for these 'English' longbows had been imported, probably from northern Spain. The first recorded instance of Yew being imported to Britain for the Longbow trade was in 1294.

At other times trees have been harvested for warfare testing. In 1953, 145 Western Yellow Pines were cut down by the US government and subsequently transported to Nevada. They were then stuck in the ground before being subjected to a nuclear blast to see what effect a nuclear bomb would have on a forest. The trees were completely flattened and burnt by the blast. One would expect that this result wasn't too much of a surprise.

Perhaps the most famous use of a tree in warfare though was during the English Civil War, when the future King Charles II hid in a Pedunculate Oak growing in the grounds of Boscobel House in Shropshire, whilst his parliamentarian pursuers searched the estate for him. Fortunately for the King, his time in the tree caused no problems for him. The tree however wasn't so lucky. It died in the 18th century following years and years of damage caused by over enthusiastic souvenir hunters who cut off bits of the tree to take back home with them as a memento to their visit to see it.

In war, everything suffers. The Danger Tree was the name given to the torn and twisted remains of a tree that had been growing in what had become no mans land in the Battle of the Somme. The tree was used as a reference point by both sides and today is marked by a replica statue commemorating the Newfoundland Regiment. This Canadian regiment was wiped out within metres of the original tree on the very first day of the battle.

Moving on to World War 2... The Changi Tree was a legendary tree growing in Singapore, it was over 70 metres in height and was believed to be many centuries old. Local folklore stated that if the tree was to fall, then so would Singapore. At the beginning of February 1942 British troops blew the tree up to prevent the advancing Japanese forces using it to range their artillery. Within a few days, Singapore had fallen to the Japanese in what was described by Winston Churchill as the 'largest capitulation' in British military history.

Perhaps the most horrific use of trees in warfare was that seen in the conflicts of South East Asia in the 1970s. A Chankiri Tree is a tree growing in what have become known as the Killing Fields in Cambodia. It is estimated that the Khmer Rouge killed 2,000,000 people between 1975 and 1979. Chankiri Trees were used to kill children; to save bullets, soldiers would smash the children's heads against the trunks of the trees to murder them.

Trees can also be extremely resilient, their survival against all odds can be seen as a beacon of hope in very dark times. In 1945, the Americans detonated an atom bomb in the skies above Hiroshima in Japan. 80,000 people were killed immediately and over 70% of the city's buildings were completely destroyed. Despite growing less than 2kms from the centre of the explosion, six Ginkgo trees somehow survived, all around them was complete devastation, but even though they were badly charred and damaged the trees soon recovered and are still alive today.

The six Ginkgoes were not the only survivors though. Throughout the obliterated city, dozens of trees somehow survived and as they recovered over the years, so too did the city. The trees are now known as Hibakujumoku, literally meaning survivor tree. These survivor trees are the following species:

Scientific Name	Common Name
Aphananthe aspera	Muku Tree
Catalpa bignonioides	Indian Bean Tree
Celtis sinensis	Japanese Hackbery
Chaenomeles speciosa	Japanese Quince
Cinnamomum camphora	Camphor Tree
Citrus natsudaidai	Amanatsu
Diospyros kaki	Japanese Persimmon
Eucalyptus melliodora	Yellow Box Eucalyptus
Euonymus japonicas	Japanese Spindle
Ficus carica	Fig Tree
Firmiana simplex	Chinese Parasol Tree
Ginkgo biloba	Ginkgo
Ilex rotunda	Kurogane Holly

Juniperus chinensis	Chinese Juniper
Lagerstroemia indica	Crape Myrtle
Melia azedarach	Chinaberry
Neolitsea sericea	Shirodamo
Nerium oleander	Oleander
Persea thungbergii	Japanese Bay
Pinus thungbergii	Japanese Black Pine
Platanus orientalis	Oriental Plane
Prunus mume	Japanese Apricot
Prunus x yedoensis	Yoshino Cherry
Robinia pseudoacacia	Black Locust
Salix babylonica	Weeping Willow
Salix chaenomeloides	Giant Pussy Willow
Tilia miqueliana	Bohdi Tree
Trachycarpus fortune	Chusan Palm
Ziziphus jujube	Jujube

There are other survivor trees to be found, two of which are in America. One of these is an American Elm growing in Oklahoma. It was almost completely destroyed by the Oklahoma bombing in 1995, in which 168 people lost their lives. The tree started to sprout new shoots the following year and is now a healthy thriving tree once again. It now forms a symbolic part of the national memorial commemorating the victims of the atrocity.

A Callery Pear tree growing in New York, is the other survivor tree. The tree grew beside the World Trade Centre, which was completely destroyed in the September 11th terrorist attacks of 2001. Although completely buried in rubble and extensively damaged, the tree is now back to full health and forms part of the national memorial to all those who died in the terrorist attacks.

Moving on to a lighter note, trees have often been used as a method of communication, particularly between the sexes. In parts of northern Poland, it is traditional for boys to chase girls on Easter Monday, whipping their legs with Juniper branches. Apparently this brings luck in love to the girls for the future. In the present, the sharp needles of the Juniper probably bring them a sore rash.

In Victorian Britain, a male suitor would give a lady a sprig of Dogwood as a sign of affection, if she returned it to him it would signify indifference, but if she kept it, it showed there was a mutual attraction. I can't help thinking that it would have been easier to just talk...

The Jujube tree's flowers have a sweet smell that is believed to make people fall in love. In the Himalayas, boys wear the flowers on their hats to make girls fall in love with them. Is this the natural equivalent to aftershave?

Using trees in this way may seem a bit silly, but it is nothing compared to these other uses. If you were off to hunt a vampire, you had to make sure that you had the right equipment. According to Eastern European folklore, the stake used to kill a vampire must be made of Hawthorn. Now you know.

Bird Cherry, native to Britain and other parts of Europe, was believed to ward off the plague. Bark from the tree was placed at the door of a house to keep the deadly disease away. Although modern medical opinion would state that it is probably best not to rely on this method.

Ancient Greeks used to divine the thoughts of the gods by listening to the rustling leaves of an Oak tree. Not sure what they did in the winter.

Legend has it that if you walk backwards ten times around the large Yew in the churchyard of Stoke Gabriel in Devon, you will be granted a wish. In reality though, you are more likely to trip over.

These silly beliefs do, bizarrely, continue today, as can be seen by this example. An unfortunate Hawthorn tree, near Ardmaddy in Scotland, is known as a wishing tree. People who hoped to make their wishes come true, would hammer a coin in to the bark of the tree as they made their wish. The tree, which is thought to have many thousands of coins embedded in its trunk, is now dead. Most of the coins hammered in to it contain copper and copper is extremely poisonous to trees. If the tree could have made just one wish, it would probably have wished that people stopped poisoning it.

Otzi the Iceman, the mummified corpse found in the Alps in 1991, had with him some wooden handled tools, his knife had a handle made from Ash and he also had a quiver of arrows made from Dogwood. This indicates that over 5,000 years ago (when Otzi was alive) people had a sound understanding of the different properties and therefore uses of the timber from different types of tree. Something that, sadly, we have now largely forgotten.

This knowledge of the properties of the timber from different types of tree has served us well over the years. Most of the pilings that form the foundations of Venice are made from Alder, the timber of which is extremely resistant to rot when immersed in water. If Oak or Beech or Pine etc had been used, then Venice would long ago have tumbled into the lagoon.

Going back to Otzi the iceman, he also had Sloes from the Blackthorn tree in his stomach. He obviously didn't have a sweet tooth!

Even older than Otzi, a fishing net made from Willow that dates back to 8300BC is one of the earliest surviving manufactured items.

Other old uses for timber is sometimes reflected in the scientific names of the tree. The Rowan tree has clusters of orange red berries that it produces every autumn, these prove extremely popular with wild birds and mankind has long exploited this. The berries were traditionally used as bait in bird traps. The Latin name for the tree is Sorbus aucuparia, the second part of this name is a derivative of the Latin for bird (avis) and catching (capere).

Trees don't just produce timber, lots of other products have been exploited by us for thousands of years. The oldest known surviving Hindu manuscripts, dating from around 1800BC, are written on Birch tree bark.

Birch bark has other ancient uses. The earliest piece of chewing gum ever found was a piece of Birch bark tar. It dates back over 5,000 years and was found in Finland complete with tooth marks in. It is not known if it was found stuck on a pavement.

The trees themselves can be used without anything being harvested. Tanzlinde is German for Dance Lime and refers to Lime trees that have been pruned and trained to form a densely spread canopy under which people can dance. They can be found throughout Germany and Switzerland, with many of the trees dating back many centuries.

Our use of trees led to our cultivation of them. The Fig tree is one of the first plants to be have been deliberately cultivated by humans, this cultivation is arguably the first evidence of agriculture in human society.

Wild Almonds are very bitter to the taste and contain enough cyanide compounds to prove fatal after only eating a few dozen of them in one go. At some point we discovered that the occasional tree produced sweeter types of nut, containing far less cyanide compounds. Using these aberrant trees we started to cultivate the Almond tree to produce the sweet, and non fatal, nut we use today. How this process occurred or started is unknown, but one would presume that those that made the mistakes didn't live long enough to tell anyone.

Cultivation of trees can be very lucrative indeed. The Minoan civilisation of Crete became wealthy on the back of the commercial Olive trade over 5,000 years ago.

Of course, where this is value, there always seems to be corruption. The genus name Theobroma means food of the gods. There are several species within this genus, but the one that led to the name is the Cocoa Tree, the source of chocolate. The Aztecs valued the cocoa beans so highly that they used them as currency; there is even evidence to suggest that people produced counterfeit beans, possibly the earliest example of currency counterfeiting.

The value in a tree's product has led to diplomatic incidents. The Chinchona tree of South America is the source of Quinine. Until the recent advent of modern drugs, quinine was the only reliable treatment against Malaria. The natives of Peru and Bolivia were well aware of the trees properties and had made it illegal to take the seeds of the species out of the country. But British explorers smuggled out seeds to establish plantations in their Indian colonies where Malaria was rife. This caused a diplomatic feud, but undoubtedly saved many lives.

Modern cultivation of trees doesn't just produce tree products though. The Northern Catalpa of North America is also known as the Worm Tree, a name given to it by fisherman. The fisherman deliberately plant the species in order to harvest it for the caterpillar of the Catalpa Moth. The caterpillar is widely considered to be the best live bait for fishing. Although it is unlikely that the Catalpa Moth concurs.

According to the US Forest Service, properly planted trees around a large building can lead to a reduction in its air conditioning needs by up to 30%. It is believed that a healthy growing tree has an overall cooling effect on its immediate area equivalent to about ten domestic air conditioner units operating for twenty hours a day.

Of course, we have long known the benefits of the shade of a tree, Hippocrates taught medicine to his students on the Greek island of Kos, in the shade of a large Oriental Plane. If you visit Kos today, you will find the Tree of Hippocrates standing proudly, casting large amounts of shade on to the ground beneath. However, this can't be the tree used by Hippocrates, he died around 2,500 years ago and the tree is only about 500 years old.

The shade of a tree as a classroom is not uncommon. During the American Civil War, Mary Smith Peake taught newly liberated slaves under a large Southern Live Oak in Virginia. Once the war was over, people gathered under the tree to hear the first reading of President Lincoln's Emancipation Proclamation. The tree is now known as the Emancipation Oak.

Leaders have also used the shade of a tree for other important acts. The Ankerwycke Yew in Berkshire is believed to be around 1,400 years old. This means that it would already have been a large tree when King John signed the Magna Carta in 1215 on the site where the tree grows. It is possible that the document was actually signed under the tree.

Another leader who supposedly took benefit from the shade of a Yew tree is Julius Caesar. The Belgian town of Lo has a large Yew tree growing there that is designated as a national monument. Known as Caesarboom, it is believed that the Roman leader, on his way to invade Britain in 55BC, tied his horse to it before having a quick nap himself in the shade of the canopy. Presumably his horse didn't browse any of the tree's foliage which is extremely poisonous to horses...

To celebrate his victory in the battle of Vienna, the Polish king, King Jan III Sobieski rested under the Bartek Oak in 1683. Before moving on, he hid a captured Turkish Sabre, an early type of firearm and a bottle of wine within the hollow trunk of the tree to commemorate the occasion. The tree, estimated at being around 700 years old, is now one of Poland's most celebrated trees.

Caesar and King Jan were victorious, others using the shade of trees before a clash haven't been quite so fortunate. In 1549, upset at the enclosure of common lands, Robert and William Kett led a rebellion to nearby Norwich. They gathered their men under a large Oak tree, since known as Kett's Oak, before marching on the city. The rebellion ultimately failed and both

William and Robert were hung for their efforts. The Oak lives on and can still be seen today.

On a happier note, the Romanian poet, Mihai Eminescu, took advantage of the dense shade cast be a Silver Lime tree in Iasi to write many of his works. The tree is now a national monument.

The shade of another tree, this time in America, was witness to the signing of the Buttonwood Agreement, a document that led to the setting up of the New York Stock Exchange in 1792. So called because the agreement was signed in the shade of a Buttonwood Tree (*Platanus occidentalis*) that was growing on Wall Street at the time.

Instead of the shade of a tree, other people have exploited the interior. The large trunks of Baobabs gradually hollow out, forming cavernous spaces within the still living tree. These have been used as homes, sometimes as prisons and, in South Africa as a bar complete with wine cellar. Other popular uses have been as places to store the dead and as reservoirs for the village. Presumably not at the same time though.

Similarly, the Baobab's close relative, the Baob in Australia have also been exploited as holding cells for convicts being transported around the country. At least two examples have been well documented as being the night time prisons for convicts as they were marched across the land.

The fruits of trees have lots of uses of course, many beneficial, but some are exploited by man for other, more nefarious reasons. *Cerbera odollam* is a tree that grows in India. It has the unfortunate common name of Suicide Tree due to the extreme toxicity of it's fruit. It has been used for centuries by people wanting to end their life and, also, by people wanting to end someone else's. In just one India state alone, it was believed to be the cause of death of more than 500 people in just ten years. It is likely that most of these were actually murder, not suicide.

The toxin found within *Cerbera odollam* is very hard to detect in autopsies, thus explaining the popularity of it among murderers. This hasn't gone unnoticed by scriptwriters, in episode 9 of the last series of the BBC TV programme New Tricks, one of the protagonists had used the fruit of the tree to murder his wife.

India has another very poisonous tree. The Strychnine Tree is, surprisingly, the source of the deadly toxin Strychnine, which is obtained from the seeds of the fruit. This deadly poison was, in Victorian times, believed to be a stimulating tonic, said to have a similar effect to strong coffee. For some reason though, the practice of drinking it died out...

Victorians had many tree related obsessions. Queen Victoria herself had one about the Purple Mangosteen of Malaysia, the fruit of which is famously good to eat. She even offered a reward of £100 (about £10,000 in today's money) to anyone who could supply her with a fresh supply of the fruit. An American food critic, writing at the time, described the fruit as "so thrilling, intoxicatingly luscious" that he would "rather eat one than a hot fudge sundae" – guessing they are quite nice then!

Often, human obsession with a tree can lead to problems for it. Red Stinkwood, a member of the Cherry family, has bark that has long been valued medicinally. It is used to treat a wide variety of conditions, from Malaria through to lack of appetite and Gonorrhoea through to insanity. As a result, the bark is highly prized and the over harvesting of it has led the tree to become endangered.

Trees can sometimes become associated with people. At times this association can be light hearted. Take Bogey's Tree growing on the 12th hole of the golf course at the exclusive Riviera Country Club in California. It is one of several trees that surround the green and proved to be such a problem for one past member that it was named after him. He was called Humphrey Bogart.

But it is not just actors that have this association with trees on golf courses. In 1956, the then president of the United States, Dwight D. Eisenhower, got so infuriated with a Loblolly Pine that was growing on the 17th hole of the Augusta National Golf Club, that he told the club's chairman that it must be immediately felled. Thankfully, the most powerful man in the western world was ignored. The tree still stands. Eisenhower presumably went away to concentrate on his swing.

Sometimes a tree's association with a person can be mysterious. In 1835, in Alabama in the United States, Charles Boyington was executed for the murder of Nathanial Frost. He had always maintained that he wasn't guilty of the crime and assured all who would listen that should he be executed, a mighty Oak would grow from his heart as proof of his innocence. A few years after his death, an Oak tree started growing from his grave and continues to grow today.

At other times, the association of a person with a tree can be tragic. A Horse Chestnut growing in Amsterdam in the Netherlands, was mentioned by Anne Frank in her diary. The tree became known as the Anne Frank tree and became a focal point for remembering this ultimately doomed young girl. Sadly though, Horse Chestnuts are not known for their longevity and in 2007 the local council declared the tree unsafe and that it needed to be felled as it was in danger of collapse. A protest group was formed and an expensive court injunction was won to prevent the felling of the tree. The protestors then spent more money carrying out various works that they said would safeguard the tree. In 2010, less than three years after the council said it was unsafe, the tree collapsed damaging several nearby buildings.

Trees can become popular destinations for visitors and are then rightly valued. The Major Oak in Nottinghamshire is the most visited tree in Britain due to its association with the legend of Robin Hood. An estimated 900,000 people visit the tree every year, bringing considerable income to the local area.

In New Zealand, there are two huge Kauri Trees growing on the North Island. They are named Tane Mahuta and Te Matua and are highly valued by the people of this country. They attract over 50,000 visitors a year and this has helped to protect these venerable giants. In 2013, during a severe drought, a watercourse was diverted to the area by the local authorities, to provide 10,000 litres of water to the trees as they were showing signs of dehydration.

Other tree tourist attractions include the Tree of Forty Fruits, a tree that produces forty different fruits sequentially throughout the spring and summer. The artist Sam Van Aken created the tree by grafting forty buds from different members of the Prunus (Cherries, Almonds, Peaches etc) family on to a root stock. The tree proceeded to produce forty branches each bearing different blossoms and fruits.

Another tree tourist attraction can be found in Australia. The Karri is a type of Eucalyptus that is famed for its great height, regularly growing to over 80 metres tall. One tree is named the

Dave Evans Bicentennial Tree and has a viewing platform constructed in it, 75 metres above the ground. Visitors reach this platform by climbing 165 metal spikes that are hammered into the trunk forming very narrow steps all the way up the tree. It is estimated that only about a fifth of visitors that set off to climb it make it to the platform, the rest turn back.

If hammering metal spikes into a tree sounds a bit extreme, it is nothing compared to the tourist attraction that is the Chandelier Tree. This tree is a large Coast Redwood growing in California in the USA. The tree became famous in the 1930s when Charlie Underwood carved a tunnel through the trunk big enough to enable a car to be able to be driven through it. Amazingly the tree is still alive today and can still be driven through, although it will cost you $5 to do so.

Other trees become attractions as monuments, we have already mentioned the various survivor trees, but there are two more that hold a significance to many. An Elm tree growing in Manhatton, New York, was the setting for the founding of the Hare Krishna religion in America. In 1966 the first outdoor chanting ritual outside of India was held under the tree. The tree has subsequently become an important religious site to followers of this religion.

The General Grant tree is a huge Giant Sequoia growing in California. In 1926, the then president, Calvin Coolidge, declared it to be the world's Christmas tree. Since then it has been declared as something more sombre. In 1956 President Eisenhower declared it as a national shrine to all those who have died in war.

Not all tree attractions grow in easily accessible areas. The 'Tree of Life' in Bahrain, is a 400 year old *Prosopis cineraria* tree that is growing in the middle of the Arabian Desert, surrounded by miles and miles of sand. Despite this, it has become a major tourist attraction getting over 50,000 visitors a year.

Unfortunately, not all trees growing in deserts fare so well when there are people about. The Tenere Tree was an Acacia tree growing in the middle of the barren and inhospitable Sahara desert. It was believed to be the most isolated tree in the entire world, with no other tree growing within 250 miles of it. However, in 1973, it was knocked over by a drunk truck driver. It has now been replaced by a metal sculpture.

Just because a tree is famous and revered it doesn't mean that it is safe. The Senator was the name of a huge Bald Cypress tree that grew in Florida. The well known tree was estimated to be around 3,500 years old and nearly forty metres tall. In 2012, an American called Sarah Barnes killed it when she decided to set light to it.

Naming a tree can lead to some protection for it, you would particularly expect that the person naming the tree would be one of those wanting to ensure it's longevity. Sadly, as this story shows, that is not always the case. The Mother of the Forest was the name of a massive Giant Sequoia growing in California. It was discovered in 1852 by George Gale and measured 98 metres in height and was estimated to be 2,500 years old. So amazed was he by the tree, George gave it the impressive name, before proceeding to strip all the bark off to apparently keep as a souvenir. This rather stupid act killed the tree.

Sometimes a name isn't a good thing. The Red Forest in the Ukraine was once a healthy woodland growing in the vicinity of Chernobyl nuclear power station. When the Chernobyl disaster occurred in 1986 the trees were all killed by massively high doses of radiation and turned the reddish brown colour which gives this unfortunate woodland it's name today. The site remains one of the most contaminated areas in the world.

To conclude this chapter of trees and their often fraught relationship with Humans is a tale illustrating how our ignorance when it comes to trees has a long history. The Madagascar Man-eating Tree gained notoriety in the 1870s when several newspapers throughout the world published an account of it consuming a human that had been sacrificed to it by a local tribe. Expeditions were even organised to go and find this carnivorous tree. The story continued for some years and was given greater credence when, in 1925, the American politician Chase Osborn published a book in which he stated that the tree did indeed exist (this was a man that nearly became vice-president...). The original account of the human sacrifice was actually taken from a fictional piece of writing and, obviously, had no basis in fact. This, of course, was no obstacle to people believing that the Madagascar Man-eater was out there lying in wait...

Myriad of Usefulness

"Someone is sitting in the shade today, because someone planted a tree a long time ago."

Warren Buffet

We use trees for all sorts of things. Timber is, of course, the obvious use, but we use them for so much more, everything from nappies through to headache cures. As previously mentioned, trees can be very different from one another and this difference means that the uses that each particular species can be put to could be completely different to the potential uses of the tree growing next to it. This chapter looks at some of the uses, but there are so many more.

One of the most popular uses of a tree is, of course, as a Christmas Tree. The practice of bringing a tree in to your home at Christmas dates back many centuries, but it was in Germany in the 19th century that it became a popular and fashionable thing to do, especially amongst the upper classes. It is often thought that Prince Albert (a German aristocrat) brought the tradition with him when he married Queen Victoria, but this isn't true. In 1800, George the third's German wife introduced a Christmas tree at a party and the royal family continued to have Christmas trees each year, including in 1832 when the then 13 year old future Queen Victoria described two of them in her diary.

The Norway Spruce is often described as being the traditional Christmas tree, but actually it was the Silver Fir that was first used as such. The foliage gives a much more 'decorated' appearance than the dull green of the Norway Spruce, it is also a lot less prickly!

In America, Christmas trees are just as popular, but they have a different suite of species to choose from. The Fraser Fir is their most popular tree and it has the distinction of being used as the White House's tree more times than any other species.

Apart from Christmas trees, there are many uses of trees in the superstitions and belief systems of the world. Elder is a common small tree found in most parts of Britain and, according to belief, they are protected by the Elder Mother. Before you can cut an Elder tree down, or even prune a branch from one, you are supposed to ask her permission, otherwise she will exact her revenge...

The Elder has long been associated with witches too. The trouble is, the association is somewhat confused. Some say that having an Elder tree near your house will ward off witches, whilst others say that witches are prone to congregate around them. Nice and clear then.

Many trees are associated with death. In the Chinese festival of Qingming, the dead are allowed to return to earth and wander about. If you don't fancy one of them wandering into your house you can ward them off by tying a Willow branch to your front door. Phew!

But you don't want to be doing that in Japan. According to Japanese tradition, ghosts appear where Willow is found!

The Muhugwe Tree of Africa not only produces good, usable timber, but also an aromatic and flammable oil that is harvested and then exported to India where it is used in traditional cremation ceremonies.

The doors of St. Peter's Basilica in the Vatican are made from the wood of the Mediterranean Cypress, a tree that is known as the drama tree in Mexico due to its propensity to bend dramatically in the slightest wind. Not only is this tree a drama queen, but it is also a symbol of mourning. In Ancient Greece, houses would be adorned with branches of it when a member of the household died. Even today, throughout the Mediterranean region, the tree is the main species found growing in cemeteries.

To return to Christmas and the story of the three kings, everyone knows what presents they brought, but, apart from the gold, many of us don't really know what they are. Frankincense is used as a high quality incense, it is actually tree sap from a species called the Olibanum tree of east Africa and the Arabian peninsula. Likewise with Myrrh, another resinous sap, this time tapped from the tree *Commiphora myrrha*.

Resinous sap of trees has been used for millennia for a huge variety of uses. This included sap from the always majestic looking Cedar of Lebanon that was used by the ancient Egyptians in the mummification process.

Meanwhile, an extract from the very resinous sap of Maritime Pine is known as Rosin. This has had a very wide range of uses over the years and is nowadays used for improving the sound that violin strings make, once applied to the strings the musical notes are much clearer in tone. Rosin is also used to remove excess hair from the ear canals of dogs. It is not known if doing this allows the dog to distinguish between untreated violin strings and ones that have been treated.

The sap of another species of tree, the Dragon Tree, is red in colour and is said to resemble the blood of dragons. The tree is a native of the Canary Islands and the dragon's blood sap has been used on the islands to make things as diverse as varnish and toothpaste.

Many indigenous peoples were intuitively in touch with the trees around them, enabling them to use specific trees for specific purposes. A good example of this involves the Lodgepole Pine. This American conifer is so called because of its use by native Americans in the construction of their Tipi. The tribes of the plains would travel long distances to source and harvest the straight, strong, but relatively lightweight stems of the Pine that could be found growing in mountainous areas.

Native Americans exploited young trees so that they would grow in a such a way as to help them in later years. The shoots of the Southern Live Oak are very pliable and this was exploited by various tribes who would bend and twist them so that they grew into a variety of shapes that would help them demarcate their trails. A sort of living signpost.

Another way these resourceful tribes would use a tree relates to the Ohio Buckeye (an American relation of the Horse Chestnut). The seeds (Conkers) would be crushed up into a mash like substance and then thrown into natural pools on a river system. The various toxins in the seeds would be released by the crushing process and these toxins would cause any fish within the pool to become stunned and float to the surface where they could be easily gathered.

Another conker bearing tree, the Indian Horse Chestnut, was used in a more direct way for food. The conkers of this species, which as the name suggests originates in India, were traditionally crushed up into a flour that was then used to make chapattis and halwa (a sweet dessert).

The Maoris of New Zealand held the Totara Tree in high esteem, worshiping many individuals. This didn't stop them felling the trees though. Many of the large ones were felled to make giant canoes, including one canoe that could seat 100 rowers, all made from the single trunk of one tree.

Other uses by native peoples have included a form of clock that could also be used to make tattoos! The Candlenut Tree grows in many places around the world, on the islands of Hawaii the large seeds were not only burnt as a form of light producing candle (the seeds have a very high oil content), but they could also be used as a way of measuring time. The seeds burn consistently, each one lasting for about 15 minutes, they would be strung together and one end would be lit. People could time how long things took by counting how many nuts were burnt in the process. The then charred seeds could be ground up to form an ink which the native islanders used to create their intricate tattoos.

Having tattoos is one thing, but making sure your hair looked good was also important. The Aboriginal tribes of Australia used to harvest the flower spikes of a tree called the Coast Banksia and turn them into hairbrushes.

To return to the Elder, when it wasn't being used to attract or repel witches it was being used to keep flies off horses. Elder flowers (as used in the cordial) would traditionally be tied to the manes of horses to keep flies from bothering the animal.

Another use of Elder is more intricate. The soft pith that is found inside the branches of this tree was once used by watchmakers to clean their tools before undertaking delicate work.

Often found growing near Elder, the Spindle tree is often overlooked these days, but in the past the tree was very important in the wool processing industry. The wood of the Spindle is very hard and can hold a very sharp point, making it idle to make the spindles for the wool processors. It is also responsible for pricking Sleeping Beauty's finger and sending her to sleep for a 100 years. Apparently.

Another tree that can apparently hold a point is the Yew. A spear head made of the wood was found at Clacton on Sea in Essex by archaeologists in 1911. When carbon dated it turned out that the wood was 450,000 years old. Unsurprisingly this is the oldest wooden spear ever found in the British Isles.

The properties of a tree's timber often guide how we have used it in the past. The first aeroplane, the Wright brothers flyer, was made from Sitka Spruce wood. The timber of this conifer has a very high strength to weight ratio, making it ideal for lightweight construction where strength is needed. A piece of the timber used in that first plane even made it to the moon in 1969 when the crew of Apollo 11 took it with them on their historic flight.

Some timber is strong and heavy. The wood of the White Oak is the favoured material for making Japanese martial art weapons such as the Bokken and the Jo. If hit by one, it is you that is going to break, not the wood.

The seeds of trees can also be equally diverse when it comes to their properties. The Foxglove Tree of China has very soft lightweight seeds. Before the invention of modern day packaging, such as polystyrene, they were used by Chinese exporters as a packaging material, especially in the shipment of ceramics. The use of this natural packing inadvertently led to the tree spreading westwards along rail and road routes as the 'packaging material' was spilt on route.

At the opposite end of the seed spectrum is the Ivory Palm of South America, the seeds of which are very, very hard. The seeds are white and resemble Elephant ivory, often being called vegetable ivory. They have been used as a much more ethical substitute, especially in the manufacture of billiard balls.

Billiard balls may not be so popular these days, but the seeds and fruits of trees are still very widely used. The fruit of the tree *Psidium guajava* is the Guava, long used in traditional medicines, it is now more widely known as a scent additive in many shampoo products.

Scent additives in shampoo is one thing, but what about in the perfume industry? The Black Hemlock, sometimes called the Mountain Hemlock, is an American species of conifer that is used in the production of scents. One of the top 100 scents in the world, Ormonde Woman, is made from an oil that is extracted from the sap of the tree.

As we are back on the subject of sap, mention has to be made of rubber. Natural rubber is the latex made from the sap of the Para Rubber Tree that is native to Brazil. However, nowadays, most natural rubber is produced in Malaysia where the tree was introduced by the British in the 1880s, despite diplomatic protests from the Brazilians. This still rankles with the Brazilians today, who feel (perhaps rightly) that they have lost a major share of the multimillion pound rubber industry. Still, they might bounce back.

The latex like sap of trees from the *Paraquium* genus is known as Gutta-percha, a substance that, in late Victorian Britain, was used to make everything from golf balls to furniture to insulation for telephone cables. Nowadays, it is only really used in dentistry to fill tooth roots during root canal surgery.

Another part of trees that is often used is the bark itself. Perhaps the most widespread bark material in use today is cork. 300,000 tonnes of cork are produced in Europe every year by removing the outer bark of the Cork Oak. This is a process that doesn't harm the tree, which immediately starts to re-grow the outer bark. This re-growth can be harvested again after 9 years. The cork is used in a wide variety of industries, although it is best known for the corks found in wine bottles, one of the largest markets is in soundproofing and insulation as well as flooring, especially in the marine industry where it's natural buoyancy is a definite advantage!

Timber is by far the most important product that we harvest from trees. It is used to make pretty much most things. Sometimes the species of tree used for the timber isn't important, but often the timber is selected because of it's specific properties. The Red Ironwood Tree is a tropical African species, as the name suggests it produces a very hard timber. The rails of the Paris Metro were made of it, whilst the tyres of the original trains that ran on them were made from the rubber of the previously mentioned Para Rubber Tree. The trees are related to one another, belonging in the same order.

Ironwood may be hard, Balsa wood isn't. Balsa comes from a short lived, but rapidly growing tree from Central and South

America. The dried timber has a lower density than cork and therefore is impossible to sink. Unsurprisingly, it was traditionally used to make rafts. It is also well known in model making where the wood's lightness and workability are readily exploited, but it also lends itself to more hi-tech uses; the blades of most wind turbines have a core made from Balsa wood.

Balsa may be impossible to sink, but then wood floats doesn't it? Well no, not all timber floats. The name Lignum Vitae is applied to several species of tree belonging to the genus *Guaiacum* that grow in Central and Southern America. The timber is heavy, very heavy, so heavy that it actually sinks in water, it is also very strong, being the strongest known timber there is. It is used to make lawn bowls, croquet balls and cricket bails for use in windy conditions. Lignum Vitae means wood of life and refers back to its past use as a medical treatment for a variety of ailments including Syphilis.

Tropical timbers are often highly sought after. Teak is one of the most well known of these timbers and produces very fine and valuable timber. The wood has a high oil content which makes the timber more resistant to weather and water., this has led it to be used for outdoor furniture, boat building and bridge construction. The U Bein bridge in Myanmar, South East Asia, is the largest bridge in the world made entirely of Teak. Spanning Lake Taungthaman, it is 1.2kms in length.

Teak is a tropical hard wood that can be cultivated and grown in plantations far away from its natural habitat. Other tropical hardwoods cannot and it is these that are often over exploited to the severe detriment of the species. *Ocotea bullata* is a tree from South Africa, it is now strictly protected and cannot legally be felled. It produces very fine quality timber that was used to make high end furniture such as dining tables etc. The tree was severely over exploited and is now listed as a threatened species. The common name for the tree is Stinkwood and, when freshly felled, the timber absolutely stinks. Unfortunately for the tree, this wears off quickly.

The Common Ash tree produces a timber that is flexible, yet strong, making it the ideal tree for many traditional tool handles. It is also used to make the stumps in cricket, a more rigid timber would be likely to break when hit by a cricket ball at speed. The strength and flexibility of Ash is used by the Morgan Sports Car Company who use it to make the frame of the car, the timber's properties aid the suspension system of the car.

The White Willow cultivar Caerulea is also more commonly known as Cricket Bat Willow due to the fact that the timber from the tree is used to make cricket bats.

The bowls of smoking pipes are made from a beautifully grained wood called Briar Root or Bruyere. The wood is actually the roots of a small Mediterranean tree, the Tree Heather which is very closely related to the heather plants found in garden centres and on the moorlands of Britain.

The phonic qualities of some woods have been recognised, many electric guitars, including the world famous Fender Stratocaster are made from the timber of Red Alder.

Californian Incense Cedar is the mainstay of an industry that produces over 14 billion items a year and it has nothing to do with incense! It is the wood used in making pencils, over three quarters of the world's pencils are made from the timber of this species.

Some trees have specific uses, others are harvested for a vast range of products. The Sitka Spruce is a tree that surely has the widest range of products made from it. We have already mentioned its use in the making of the first aeroplane and the timber from this species still gets used in the manufacture of small planes, as well as in the building of houses where again the high strength to weight ratio is important. But there are many more uses, everything from Nappies to Nuclear! Sitka timber is used in the nose cones of Trident missiles and the wood pulp is used to create cellulose which is then used to make disposable nappies. The high cellulose content of Sitka also make it the paper tree, the pages you are reading this on will have probably originated from the tree. It is also used to make cellophane and even clothing.

You may think that this would qualify the Sitka Spruce as a super tree, but I think that title has to go instead to the Neem Tree of the Indian subcontinent. Where it grows it is very highly valued for the dense shade that it casts in areas where other trees often struggle to grow, whilst the roots of the tree help bind the poor soils and stop them being eroded away. The tree is also used as a food source, with the tender young shoots and flowers widely eaten as a vegetable. The leaves, when burnt, give off a chemical that keeps away mosquitoes, whilst the twigs are widely used as toothbrushes! A truly multipurpose tree that is exploited for so many things, without being felled.

Food is of course something else we get from trees. Whilst Camembert cheese doesn't itself come from a tree, the small round case that it comes in does. It is made of Poplar wood, the wood that is also used to make matches.

Likewise, the branches of Western Hemlock don't directly give us food, but native Alaskans have long used them to collect fish eggs. The numerous soft needles catch the eggs as they drift in the flow of the river, they also impart their flavour to the eggs as well. Fish roe with a hint of tree.

We will come back to the food in a minute, but how about a drink for starters. Many trees have been used to brew beer, the bark, needles and wood of the original Christmas tree, the Silver Fir, were widely used to make beer in Europe until relatively modern times.

Beer isn't necessarily thought of as been a health drink, but Spruce beer, which is very rich in Vitamin C, could claim to be one. Brewed from the buds, shoots and needles of various Spruce species, this beverage has a long history of being used on long distant sea voyages to help prevent scurvy amongst the crew. Captain Cook, amongst others, employed this method to keep his crew healthy during their epic voyages of exploration in the 18th century. I am sure the sailors begrudgingly accepted the offer of regular free beer...

The Wild Service Tree produces fruits that were once used to flavour beer as well. The small, pear like fruits that the tree produces are called Chequers. Chequers is the name of the British Prime Minister's official country residence, it was named this because of the prevalence of the tree in the area in which the estate was formed.

Amaretto is an Italian liqueur that has a strong almond flavour. But the majority of the kernels used in it's production are not actually almonds, they are, instead, the kernels of the closely related apricot. Apricot seeds contain just over 2% Hydrogen Cyanide. You know what to blame if you get a hangover...

The Terebinth Tree of southern Europe has a resinous sap long used to make Turpentine and is widely believed to be the earliest source of this solvent, which is used for many purposes, but is probably best known as being used to clean paint brushes. In Cyprus they have another use for it, the sap is used to make a local Brandy called Tsikoudia, which one would imagine is rather potent!

Some trees are used not for making the alcoholic drink, but for storing it. White Oak timber is the favourite wood for making barrels for maturing wine in, it is also used to age bourbon.

Trees are used to make many other drinks as well as the boozy varieties. The Kola Nut Tree of West Africa produces a nut that is used to flavour certain soft fizzy drinks. You may have heard of them.

The Amargo Tree of Central America is used as an organic insecticide to kill aphids, caterpillars and even the Colorado Potato Beetle. It is also used to flavour numerous soft drinks. Hmmm...

If it wasn't continuously picked, *Camellia sinensis* would grow in to a relatively tall tree. However, every two weeks the newly grown tips are deliberately picked from the plant, this constant picking stunts its growth considerably. *Camellia sinensis* is more commonly known as tea.

Tea is obviously a very popular drink and so is coffee, like tea it is obtained from a tree. The Mountain Coffee Tree was the first species of the genus *Coffea* to be cultivated for coffee production. It now accounts for over three quarters of all the world's coffee. Originating in Ethiopia in Africa, people first decided to cultivate the tree for human consumption after apparently watching goats copulate after they had been browsing on the leaves of the tree! Now there's a thought the next time you sit down to enjoy a coffee...

Like the Mountain Coffee Tree, many of the species of Holly growing in the world are high in caffeine, one species, *Ilex paraguariensis*, is the source of the hugely popular South American drink Maté.

The Yaupon Holly of North America was traditionally used by the native Americans to make a drink called Black Drink (I am guessing it is pretty dark!). It was drunk in purification ceremonies, the Latin name for the tree may give you a clue on just how it purified you, *Ilex vomitoria*.

Moving on to solids then, the Mastic Tree, a close relative of the afore mentioned Terebinth Tree, is cultivated on the Greek island of Chios, in the Aegean Sea, for its resinous sap known as Mastic. This has long been used as a form of chewing gum (for several thousand years), as well as a flavouring in many foods and drink. It is also used to make a high grade varnish.

Tree flowers can be used as a source of food, as mentioned earlier with the Neem Tree. In Thailand, the dried flowers of the Cotton Tree *Bombax ceiba* are used to flavour Nam Ngiao noodle soup and Kaeng Khae curry.

Tree flowers can also be used by bees in the production of honey. Sometimes with unexpected results. Honey made from some species of Rhododendron (Latin for Rose Tree) can have both a hallucinogenic and laxative effect. That really doesn't sound like a good combination!

Even flower buds have their culinary uses. Cloves are used in many dishes as well as being used to flavour that Christmas favourite, mulled wine. The clove is actually the dried flower bud of a tree called *Syzygium aromaticum* that is native to parts of Indonesia. In their homeland, they are also used to make a type of cigarette called Kretek and even as an ant repellent. One final use is as an anaesthetic for fish. So there you go, if you ever need to anaesthetise your goldfish, you know what to do!

It is mainly the fruits and seeds of trees that provide us with foodstuffs. Pine nuts, used to make pesto and also in many other culinary dishes, are raved about by the top chefs. They are the seeds found within the large cones of the Stone Pine. We have long recognised the nutritional value of these seeds, with evidence suggesting that we have been cultivating the tree for over 6,000 years.

Of course, for a fruit to form, a flower needs to be pollinated. Humans have long recognised this too. California is the largest producer of almonds in the world. Pollination of the beautiful flowers of this species of the cherry family occurs every year in February. But this doesn't just happen haphazardly, the pollination of California's almonds is the largest managed pollination event in the world. Almost half of all the beehives in America are transported from 49 states to the almond orchards allowing the bees to pollinate the trees. Must be quite a buzz.

The spice that we call Allspice is made from the dried, unripe berries of a tree called the Jamaica Pepper and is widely used in Caribbean cooking. Another use for this spice is as a deodorant!

Staying in the Caribbean, the Ackee Tree of Jamaica, a relative of the tree that gives us the lychee, produces a fruit that is officially the national fruit of that island. It is widely used in Jamaican cuisine, but if unripe it is slightly toxic and consuming it in this state can lead to a condition known as Jamaican Vomiting Sickness.

The Tamarind tree is originally from West Africa, but is now cultivated widely across the tropics. The fruits of the tree are widely used in cooking, particularly in Indian food. In Central America, the fruits are used to make sweets and here in Britain we use it to make Worcestershire Sauce. Alternatively the fruits can be used to polish brass and copper.

Literally translated, the name of the *Scorodocarpus* tree of Borneo means garlic fruit. Unsurprisingly, these fruits do indeed smell and taste of garlic, they are used in native cooking in exactly the same way that we use garlic in the west.

The genus *Diospyros* (from the ancient Greek meaning Divine Fruits) contains trees that give us such fruits as the Persimmon and Kaki, as well as trees that give us the heavy, black and valuable timber, Ebony.

One other part of a tree that deserves a mention whilst we are talking about food is the gall. Galls are produced by trees (and other plants) in response to various parasites that in some way attack the tree. The galls found on the Aleppo Oak are traditionally used to thicken stews in a similar way to using flour.

These galls are also used for medicinal purposes too. Everything from the successful treatment of toothache to the tightening of the muscles in the vagina following childbirth, has been attributed to the galls of the Aleppo Oak.

The potential medicinal properties of trees has long been known. Chewing willow bark for pain relief is a practice that dates back millennia. Hippocrates was prescribing it in 500BC, whilst ancient Egyptian texts mention it for combating fevers. In 1828, the extract Salicin was successfully isolated from the bark and in 1897, Felix Hoffman created a synthetic version for his employer. His employer was called Bayer and they named the synthetic Salicin, Aspirin. You may have heard of it!

The quest for new medicine from trees still goes on. Paclitaxel is a drug used in the treatment of various cancers. It was first created in 1962 following a plant screening trial in the USA that identified the bark of the Pacific Yew as having potential in the treatment of cancer. Initially to harvest the drug, the bark had to be stripped from the trees leading to the death of what was already a declining species. Further research continued and now the drug can be made synthetically using other species of Yew.

The resinous sap of the Silver Fir can be used to produce an oil that has medically proven soothing powers when applied in a massage.

The sap of the related Balsam Fir was once used widely in science to seal in samples on microscope slides, preserving them perfectly between two pieces of glass. On the medicine theme, it is used in a commercial cough medicine that uses the slogan "It tastes awful and it works"! There's honesty for you.

As previously mentioned, Captain Cook and many others wished to prevent scurvy from affecting their crew on long distant voyages. The bark of the Winter's Bark Tree was used to make a vitamin C rich type of tea for the sailors to drink. I bet it wasn't as popular as the Spruce beer though!

From the same genus of trees that gives us the spice Cinnamon, the Camphor Laurel produces the insecticide of the same name. The wood of this tree was widely used on the long distant voyages in the age of exploration to make trunks and storage boxes to keep moths and beetles from damaging the clothes and foodstuffs held within.

A tree called the Suicide Tree has already been mentioned in a previous chapter, but there is another tree species that shares this unfortunate moniker. This time the tree in question is *Tachigali versicolor* and it is found growing in Central America. Unlike the Suicide Tree of India however, this tree doesn't help humans kill themselves or others. No, this suicide tree really lives up to the name by committing suicide itself! The species only produces seed once and within a year of doing so, it dies and falls over leaving a perfect tree size hole in the canopy for the newly set seed to grow into. The natives of the area also harvest parts of the Central American Suicide Tree, but not for sinister purposes; they use the leaves for treating Athlete's Foot! Now you really wouldn't want to be getting confused between the two species if you were a chemist...

The Khat tree of the Arabian peninsula is widely used as a narcotic stimulant. The leaves are chewed socially and also to aid business discussions. The English author Charles Dickens described the affect of chewing Khat as being similar to drinking very strong green tea. In June 2014 the British government made it illegal to use Khat, so I guess we will be sticking to the tea in our future business discussions then.

Trees are used to produce all sorts of stimulants of course. Members of the genus *Virola* from South America produce leaves that are used to make hallucinogenic snuff. Now there's something not to be sniffed at.

Mahogany is the name of the timber produced by the three species of trees in the *Swietenia* genus. These trees are well known for producing quality wood. The seed pods though have a medicinal use, being used as a Viagra style treatment. Quality wood indeed.

And finally for this chapter, a tale of how different cultures use the same thing for different outcomes. Native Americans would use the berries of the Juniper as a female contraceptive. In Europe though, the berries of the Juniper are used to flavour the alcoholic drink, gin. The over usage of which has often led to the need for contraceptives...

Tree Biology

"All theory is grey, but the golden tree of life is ever green."

Johann Wolfgang von Goethe

The biology of trees is fascinating and extremely varied. They all might look superficially the same, but they have all evolved differently from one another. This chapter looks at trees from a biological point of view.

Mighty oaks from little acorns grow, is a saying that is very true indeed. It can be hard to imagine how a tiny seed, just 3mm in length could produce a tree over 100 metres tall, but that is what the Coast Redwood does.

Seeds have many adaptations, many of which aid them in their dispersal away from the parent tree. The seeds of Maple trees, with their 'wings' slowing them down as they drop from the tree catch the wind and can be blown some distance. This 'wing' casing on Maple seeds is also found on trees like Ash and many Elms and is called a Samara.

In World War 2, the American military used these samaras as inspiration, developing a special air drop container based on the maple seed. The container could carry almost 30kgs of equipment which would drop gently to the ground undamaged all thanks to the Maple.

Seeds don't just rely on the wind of course. Many use animals, everything from ants to elephants distribute tree seeds. Some trees have evolved to deliberately exploit particular creatures to scatter their seeds. If a tree produces red fruits, it is doing so to deliberately attract birds to disperse their seeds. Studies have shown that birds, which have good colour vision, positively select red berries over other coloured ones.

The fruits of figs are often red when ripe and these too are eaten by birds, they are also eaten by many mammals, both the birds and mammals then distribute the seeds in their droppings. A fairly typical way for a tree to pass on it's genes to the next generation. But the way the fruits of the fig are pollinated is not so typical. There are 800 or so species of Fig in the world and each and every one has co-evolved with a different species of small wasp, forming a highly intricate relationship that benefits both. The wasps act as the pollinator of the fig's flowers, which obviously benefits the tree, the wasp benefits from being able to lay its eggs within the fig itself, allowing them to develop in the safe confines of the fruit.

Many species of conifer rely on fire to distribute their seeds. The cones of these species only open after a fire has heated them sufficiently to melt the resin that bonds them shut. The fires that generate the heat to release the seeds, have also prepared the ground for the seeds to germinate in, burning away any other vegetation and leaving a fertile layer of ash behind.

The name conifer means bearing cones, yet some conifer trees, such as the Juniper and the Yew appear to have berries instead. Biologically speaking though, these aren't berries, they are arils. An aril is a growth from the seed itself that covers the seed, on

Yews and Junipers this growth is actually a highly modified cone scale making these 'berries' actually cones.

The aril of the Yew is the red fleshy part of what is commonly known as the Yew berry. It is very sweet to the taste and is probably the only part of the tree that isn't poisonous to eat. However, the seed within the aril is very poisonous and should not be digested.

The Yew is a classic example of how some trees evolve relationships with some creatures when it comes to seed dispersal, yet deter others from eating it's precious crop. The digestive system of the fruit eating birds that the Yew attracts with the red coloured fruit is relatively simple, meaning that the actual seed passes through the bird undigested. The bird having benefited from the sweet fleshy aril around the seed, then repays the favour by depositing the seed, complete with a bit of fertilizer, away from the parent tree. If mammals, including ourselves, eat the seeds our gut system will actually digest it, stopping that seed from being able to ever germinate. The tree obviously doesn't want that to happen, so it deters us mammals by making the seed poisonous. The idea being that once we have been ill from eating the seeds of the tree we won't return to do so again.

Some trees though have evolved a need for mammals to eat their seeds, rather than birds. The Guanacaste Tree in Central America is one such tree, bizarrely the seed pods of this tree resemble large ears and have led to a whole host of alternative names including the Elephant Ear Tree, Devil's Ear Tree and Ear Pod Tree. Because the seed pods are large they fall directly on to the floor below it and often accumulate there. It is believed that in the past the seeds would have been eaten by the now extinct Giant Ground Sloth and Giant Bison. The digestive process of these animals would have caused abrasion to the seed casing which is needed for the seed to actually germinate. Without the damage the seed won't germinate, which is a good thing as they would still likely be underneath the parent tree. Luckily for the tree, modern day horses and cattle fulfil the disperser's role, eating the seeds, damaging the seed case in the digestion process and then depositing the seed away from the parent tree and in a big pile of fertilizer!

Climate conditions are often very important for trees, none more so than the current tallest species, the Coast Redwood. The key weather for this giant is fog. A substantial part of the tree's water requirement comes from the water drops that coalesce on the fine foliage of the tree, where they form larger drops that then drop to the ground beneath. The fog and the subsequent drips, keep the forest floor constantly moist, ensuring that the trees have enough water. But it isn't the only way that these trees get a drink, the foliage itself is specially adapted to absorb the water in the fog, directly reducing the strain on the tree which would otherwise have to transport the water up to their very high tree tops. The tallest of all Coast Redwoods only occur in the areas prone to high occurrences of fog.

Other trees benefit from fog, but one type of tree in particular is known for making mist. The Blue Mountain Range in New South Wales, Australia, gets it's name from the smog like mist that often shrouds them on warm days, making them appear a hazy blue. The mist is made up of volatile organic compounds that have been given off by the abundant Eucalyptus trees growing in the area.

The natural distribution of tree species is, like the trees themselves, very diverse. Some have very small ranges others span continents. The British Isles are home to several species of Whitebeam that are found nowhere else in the world, some of these are restricted to individual valleys or cliff areas. These endemic species are unique to Britain, yet hardly receive any attention.

The tree with the largest natural distribution in the world is the Common Juniper, it spans right around the entire northern hemisphere.

The Common Juniper is one of just three species of conifer that are native to the British Isles, the other two are the Common Yew and the Scots Pine.

We often think of England as being the home of the Oak, but we are very 'Oak Poor' when it comes to the number of species that naturally occur here, we have just two, the Pendunculate and the Sessile. The place in the world that has the most naturally occurring Oak species is Mexico, a country that has 109 endemic Oak species found nowhere else in the world. Sadly, many of these species are critically endangered.

In total there are over 450 species of Oak scattered across the world, the majority of them are actually evergreen, retaining their leaves throughout the year.

One of the trees in Britain that just about anybody can recognise is the Common Holly. It is the sole representative of it's family in Europe, yet elsewhere in the world there are another 380 plus Holly species, the vast majority of which are found in tropical mountain areas.

Our tree fauna in the British Isles has been greatly added to over the last 2,000 or so years and many species that we assume are native are not. These include the rather badly named English Elm, which is introduced. Only one species of Elm is native to the UK and that is Wych Elm.

The first tree introduced to Britain from the newly colonised continent of North America was the Eastern Redcedar, which was brought here in 1536. It was the first of many.

The Autumn colours of many trees are a real seasonal delight. The Maple genus of trees is perhaps the one most associated with this phenomenon and it seems that the tree is going through this process to defend itself. It is believed that the red colouring of the turning leaves is caused by an antioxidant that helps the tree from sustaining cell damage as it removes the chlorophyll from the leaves.

Trees use their leaves in other forms of defence. The leaves of the Common Holly are prickly as a defence against mammalian browsers such as deer. Producing these prickles though, costs the tree in terms of energy, therefore, once the tree is tall enough to be out of reach of the browsers, it's leaves lose their prickles, saving the tree energy. This is why the upper branches on taller Holly trees bear leaves with less or no prickles on.

As you would expect, the evolutionary struggle between would be tree browsers and the trees themselves has produced many examples of how far trees will go to defend their precious leaves. Several species of Acacia have formed alliances with ants. For their part, the tree provides homes for the insects in specially adapted hollow thorns. In return the ants defend the tree from pests such as caterpillars and even large mammals, with many a browser having been put off eating the leaves of an Acacia tree by swarming ants running up their nostrils!

Other trees produce chemicals in their attempts to ward off browsers. When attacked by mammals such as Elephants, the African Mopane Tree rapidly increases the amount of tannins in the leaves making them very bitter and unpalatable. This rapidly deters the Elephant from browsing on the tree, resulting in minimal damage to it.

But that's not all. Mopane trees don't just increase their own tannin levels when browsed by Elephants, they also tell other Mopane trees nearby to do so as well. The trees release a chemical signal into the air that is then picked up by the other trees, which in turn increase the tannin levels in their own leaves. It has been observed that when the gargantuan browsers feed on Mopane trees, they only visit each tree briefly and then head upwind to the next tree in the hope that the chemical signal won't have reached it yet. This is evidence that trees actually communicate with each other and not by trunk call either.

Trees often need to defend themselves from competition from other trees as well. The best way to do this, is of course to kill off your competitors. In Britain, the most ruthless of trees is the Beech, they will even commit genocide in order to have the woodland to themselves. If a young Beech sapling becomes established in a woodland setting, it will outgrow the other species of tree present, eventually over-topping them. Their densely leaved canopy then goes to work, shading the other trees out which will cause them to eventually die, due to the lack of sunlight. To ensure that it keeps rivals even more suppressed, the tree then drops it's leaves every autumn. These leaves, as they rot down, release chemical inhibitors in to the soil that help prevent the seeds of other species from germinating. This is why Beech forests are lacking in other tree species and have very little vegetation growing underneath them, giving them their characteristic open appearance. An appearance that is purely the result of the Beech tree killing off the opposition. Beech are not alone in their murderous ways, many species of tree do the same, including the Black Walnut of North America.

All trees, to some extent, have to defend themselves from the environment in which they live. Perhaps one of the most extreme habitats for plants to grow in is salt water, as salt is extremely toxic to plants, including trees. The Mangroves are trees that live in salt water, meaning that they have had to evolve some specialist adaptations to be able to exploit this niche. The Black Mangrove deals with the salt in the sea water by expelling it through the leaves, this gives the leaves a ghostly white coating, they also have specially adapted roots called pneumatophores that stick up, above the water surface and act a bit like snorkel allowing air to get to the roots. The Red Mangroves grow strong stilt like roots keeping the main part of the tree out of the water, they have special openings on their trunks called lenticels which enable the tree to absorb air. The roots that are submerged, have a layer of suberin, a waxy substance that is found in cork, making them impermeable to salt, protecting the other parts of the tree from salt damage.

As mentioned above, suberin is also found in cork, which makes up the outer bark of the Cork Oak tree. This specialised bark isn't needed to protect the trees from salt, but from fire. Cork doesn't burn, which obviously helps protect the tree in a fire. It is also a good insulator, preventing the heat of the fire from reaching the more delicate parts of the tree underneath the outer bark shield.

Likewise the Giant Redwood is also fire resistant. It's bark isn't made of cork, but is instead incredibly fibrous forming a thick protective layer around the trunk of the tree. The Giant Redwood and the Cork Oak are great examples of convergent evolution, where unrelated species separately evolve similar features.

Another tree that has to deal with heat, as well as a severe lack of water, is the Saharan Cypress. As the name suggests, it survives in one of the most inhospitable places on Earth, the Sahara Desert in Africa, an area that gets virtually no annual rainfall. The area is so inhospitable to life that no other species of tree grows within hundreds of kilometres of the small population of 233 Saharan Cypresses that have called this incredibly harsh and sandy place home.

Trees are in a constant battle with fungal pathogens, sometimes the pathogen gets the upper hand. This is definitely the case when it comes to Elms. The virulent strain of Dutch Elm disease, a strain that has caused such devastation to the Elms of Britain, first arrived on a shipment of Elm timber from the United States of America.

Within ten years of first being detected in the UK, the virulent strain of this fungal disease had 'killed' over 20 million trees in the country. Often though, especially with English Elm, not all of the tree is killed, with some of the roots surviving. If left in situ, these roots will eventually generate suckers that will start to grow into trees. At the moment these young trees usually succumb to the disease between 15 and 25 years of age, but eventually the tree will regain the upper hand in this battle and they will once again return as the splendid large trees that once dominated parts of the British landscape.

Dutch Elm Disease has nothing to do with the Dutch, it didn't originate in the Netherlands, nor do the Dutch go about surreptitiously spreading it. The reason it has been given the name it has is because the scientists who first discovered the disease in 1921 happened to be Dutch.

Earlier, we looked at how some trees, including Acacias, go to great lengths to deter browsing. But some Acacias actually encourage it. The Knobthorn of Western and Southern Africa, produces flowers that Giraffes like to eat. The flowers, it seems are attractive to these long necked herbivores, with the animal positively selecting them. In the process of eating them the Giraffe gets pollen all over it's lips and face. When it goes to another Knobthorn tree to browse on the flowers there, it also unwittingly pollinates some of them too.

Trees have evolved all sorts of schemes to ensure that their flowers get pollinated. Some provide central heating for their would be pollinators. The flowers of the South American tree *Annona sericea* actually raise their temperature to 6°C above the ambient temperature, making them much more attractive to the insects that pollinate them. We don't normally think of plants being able to raise their own temperature, but this species of tree, and others, do.

When you are in a dense area of woodland, it can appear, with branches and trunks seemingly everywhere, that tree growth is random in character. In fact, trees exhibit a behaviour known as phototropism, in other words they grow towards sunlight. If a space in the canopy opens up, the neighbouring trees will direct their growth towards it so that they can benefit from the extra sunlight.

Conifers first appeared on Earth 300 million years ago, they dominated their world and it is likely that there were thousands of species. Today there are only 630 species of conifer in the world.

One of those species has only recently been discovered, or should I say re-discovered. Fossils of a conifer tree called *Wollemia nobilis* date back from over 120 million years ago. In 1994, in New South Wales Australia, a National Park employee discovered some living examples in a remote, unexplored canyon. The last previous known example of the tree was from a fossil which was two million years old.

Only one tree in the world has been known to produce mature albino specimens. There are 230 known Albino Coast Redwoods in the world. Because these trees lack chlorophyll (they would be green if they had it), they are unable to photosynthesise, therefore, in able to get nutrients, they have to parasitise other Coast Redwoods by grafting their roots on to the 'normal' trees. The foliage of the trees is entirely white, giving them an incredible ghostly appearance.

Although the Coast Redwood produces the very rare albino form that exists as a parasite, there is only one true parasitic type of conifer, *Parasitaxus usta*. It is found on the island of New Caledonia in the Pacific Ocean, where it taps in to the roots of other tree species, stealing the nutrients it requires.

Although incredibly rare in conifers, parasitism is exhibited by several species of tree. The Sandalwood Tree is rightly famed for producing high quality timber and is widely known in the furniture world. What is less widely known is that the tree is a member of the same order as Mistletoe, and just like Mistletoe it too is a parasite. It uses specially adapted roots to steal nutrients from other trees and shrubs that are growing nearby.

Some deciduous trees exhibit a behaviour known as Marcesense. This term describes deciduous trees that retain their dead leaves on the branches until they are knocked off by a physical force. We have long exploited this in hedging plants, with both young Beech and young Hornbeam trees which have marcesent leaves, making beautiful hedges.

Finally, The Cocoa Tree that gives us chocolate is pollinated by midges. No midges would mean no chocolate. Remember that the next time you are being bit on a warm summer's evening, it will make you feel better. Possibly.

A Miscellany of the Miscellaneous

"A sure cure for seasickness is to sit under a tree."

Spike Milligan

This chapter looks at all the other wonderful snippets of miscellany relating to trees that just didn't seem to fit in anywhere else!

The Fig that you eat is the fruit of the Common Fig Tree. Its pollinating wasp, a species called *Blastophaga psenes*, dies within the developing fruit, where it is then broken down by enzymes, giving the fig that you eat just that extra special bit of protein...

A single Pistachio Tree can produce 50kgs of Pistachios every two years. Now that sounds like a lot of nuts, until you consider that the Chinese manage to consume 80,000 metric tonnes (or 80 million kilograms) of them every single year!

Transporting such vast numbers of pistachios comes with risk. Shipments have been known to spontaneously combust in transit, due to their low water, high fat content and their propensity for self heating!

Do you know what the shell of a Cashew Nut looks like? The odds are that you don't, because the shell of the Cashew is actually toxic, which is why they are never sold in their shells.

With or without it's poisonous shell, the cashew is actually closely related to the Mango.

On the subject of tropical fruits, the Rambutan tree of South-east Asia produces the edible fruit of the same name. This name is derived from the Malay word for hair. It refers to the hairy appearance of the unpeeled fruit (the hairs are actually just unkempt spines). Meanwhile, in nearby Vietnam, the name for this fruit is Chom Chom, which translates as messy hair. Have you ever had a Chom Chom day?

We often associate flowers with nice smells, but that isn't always the case. The flowers of the American Callery Pear stink strongly of rotting fish. But those of the related Plymouth Pear, a tree native to Spain, Portugal, and France, smell of rotting scampi instead. Does this mean that there are people who are connoisseurs of rotting seafood, distinguishing with their highly skilled noses different types of fetid sea life?

On the subject of smells... The seeds of the Stink Bean Tree of South East Asia are a popular food used for many culinary purposes. The common name for the tree comes from the fact that the seed pods do have a very strong scent, which some liken to the smell of natural gas. Unsurprisingly, eating the seeds in large quantities is linked to the production of excessive flatulence!

The Holm Oak and the cultivated Hazel known as the Filbert are the most popular tree species in truffle orchards.

The genus *Prunus* has over 400 species within it, some of these produce a wide variety of edible fruits, including cherries, peaches and almonds. All members of the genus also contain varying levels of cyanide.

It is well known that the foliage of the Common Yew is very toxic. It can kill humans, cattle and horses, yet deer seem able to eat it without any harm

King Cativolcus, of what was then north east Gaul, supposedly killed himself by poisoning, rather than surrender to the advancing armies of the Roman Empire. He apparently made himself a concoction brewed from the leaves of the Common Yew tree.

The Irish Yew is a variety of the Common Yew that exhibits fastigiate (or upright) growth. They are very popular in our churchyards and in gardens throughout Britain and Ireland. All of these are descendants of one tree that was planted as a sapling in the year 1740 in Florencourt in County Fermanagh, Northern Ireland. The original tree is still alive today.

A Common Yew tree growing in Estry in the Normandy region of France, is believed to be one of the oldest trees in the country. The tree's large hollow trunk is so capacious that it can hold up to 30 people within it.

In a show of neighbourly one-upmanship though, the nearby La Haye de Routot has a small chapel, called the Chapelle de Sainte Anne, carved into the trunk of one of their Common Yew trees.

But surely the winner of this French tree status symbol battle has to be the Chene Chapelle or Chapel Oak that is found in Allouville – Bellefosse in northern France. It doesn't just have one chapel, oh no, it has two of them within its hollow interior. They were created in the year 1669 and mass is still held in them two times a year. Access to these chapels is provided by a wonderful spiralling staircase that goes up and around the trunk of the tree.

There are three tree seeds that are mentioned in the bible; the Pistachio, the Walnut and the Almond.

The beautiful Judas Tree of Southern Europe and Western Asia is supposed to be the tree in which Judas Iscariot hung himself, hence it's name. However, the truth is that the tree took it's name from the French Arbre de Judée which means Tree of Judea, an area of the Middle East where the tree is abundant.

There are many other folklore tales about trees and hangings. In England, it was believed that the devil hung his very own mother in a Rowan tree.

Near Bcheale in Lebanon, there is a grove of 16 Olive Trees that according to legend are believed by some to be the source of the Olive branch that a Dove carried back to Noah's Ark following the biblical flood.

In the sixth century BC, Prince Siddhartha sat in the shade of a large Fig tree. Whilst doing so he received enlightment and from then on was known as the Buddha. From this, the tree species under which he sat received the name of the Sacred Fig.

According to Chinese Folklore, it is a very bad idea to use the timber of the Japanese Pagoda Tree in the construction of your house. This is because demons are apparently attracted to it.

Meanwhile in Africa, a tropical hardwood tree called Iroko produces good quality timber that has earned it the trade name of African Teak even though it is completely unrelated to Teak. If you are superstitious though, you might want to stick to the original teak for your furniture needs – according to African folklore, the tree is home to a spirit, if you have the misfortune of seeing this spirit, you will very quickly become insane and die!

On the Greek island of Skopelos in the Aegean Sea, it is said that whoever plants a Walnut tree, will die when the tree can see the sea. Unsurprisingly it is not a tree that does well in the local garden centre.

Meanwhile, in Western Serbia, the head of the household would traditionally crack open a walnut on Christmas Day. If the nut came out good, it supposedly foretold a prosperous year to come. However, if the nut turned out to be bad, the head of the household had to instantly run around the outside of their house three times, pleading with god not to listen to someone called Jack as, and I quote, they were full of cack!

On the Isle of Man, it was thought that if a young woman placed the leaf of an Ash tree in her left shoe, she would then immediately meet her future husband. What happened if she put the leaf in her right shoe has not been recorded.

Merlin's Oak was an old Oak tree growing in the town of Carmarthen in Wales. Legend had it, that the tree marked the birthplace of the wizard Merlin who is said to have made the prophecy that when the Oak fell down, so Carmarthen would fall too. The tree died in 1856. Carmarthen didn't.

The Oak of Mamre, sometimes known as Abraham's Oak, can be found in Palestine in the Middle East. It has been estimated at being over 5,000 years old. According to legend, the tree will die when the Antichrist arrives. The tree died in 1996. Who do you know that was born in 1996?

The Ashoka Tree of India is a sacred tree in both Hinduism and Buddhism. The flowers of this member of the Pea family are highly decorative and are treated as religious offerings by both religions. According to folklore, the trees are said to produce more showy flowers if the tree has been beaten, prior to blossoming, by young women. Interestingly enough, there is no scientific evidence available to back this claim up.

Baobabs are great trees and have featured many times within these pages. Their shape has long been a source of fascination. The twisted fine branches atop the swollen trunks resemble roots rather than your typical tree branches and many folklore tales have evolved to explain them. My favourite states that the original Baobab was a beautiful tree, but the tree was vain and thought itself far superior than others as a result of its beauty. To punish it, the gods uprooted it and planted it upside down.

The large trunks of these mighty Baobabs have evolved to act as reservoirs. The timber within is actually very spongy in structure, allowing the tree to store large quantities of water in the brief rainy season. It can then utilise this stored water when the long drought comes.

Allow me one final mention of these great trees. The Baobab's fruit is, in modern day parlance, a real super food. It contains 50% more Calcium than Spinach does and has three times the amount of Vitamin C than an Orange does!

A Sycamore tree growing along Hadrian's Wall in Northumberland in the North of England, is supposedly Britain's most iconic tree. The tree growing in a gap between two small hills, sits perfectly in the landscape and has been the backdrop of many a photo. It was also used as a backdrop in the opening shots of the Kevin Costner movie, Robin Hood Prince of Thieves.

The Midland Oak that grew near Leamington Spa in England, was said to mark the exact middle of the country. The original tree died in 1967, but a successor, grown from an acorn from the original tree, is now growing in its place.

The Big Tree is a name given to a Southern Live Oak growing in Texas in America. It has become a tourist attraction in it's own right and has become one of the most famous trees in the United States. It has been estimated that this tree has survived over fifty major hurricanes, dozens of serious floods and tens of wildfires.

Live Oaks are very popular trees in the United States and in 1934, Dr Edwin Lewis Stephens founded the Live Oak Society to advance the culture, preservation and appreciation of Southern Live Oak across America. The society still continues today, the current president is probably the oldest president of any society in the world; it is a 1500 year old Southern Live Oak named the Seven Sisters Oak.

The USS Constitution is probably the most famous war ship in American naval history. It was built in 1797 using Southern Live Oak timber, this wood is known for being extremely hard and the ship soon earned the nickname of 'Old Ironsides' as it withstood intense canon fire during the war of 1812 to defeat five British navy ships. The United States navy considered Southern Live Oak to be such an important timber tree they established many plantations of it to keep them well supplied. They still own many of these plantations today.

The Norway Spruce is generally recognised as being the true Christmas Tree, despite it not being the original species used. As a thank you gesture by the people of Norway, the Norwegian government supplies large Norway Spruce trees to Edinburgh, London, New York and Washington every Christmas to thank those countries for the help given to Norway in World War Two.

If trees could talk, is a saying often murmured when people see large specimens, it certainly would be interesting if one of the largest Sessile Oaks in Britain could talk. Named the Queen Elizabeth Oak, this tree in West Sussex witnessed the ascendancy to the throne of Queen Elizabeth the First. On the 17th November 1558, Elizabeth's half sister, the then Queen Mary died, Elizabeth was stood beside the tree when she was told the news.

From the Elizabethan Age to the Space Age. On the 1971 Apollo 14 space mission, 500 seeds from five different trees were on board the spacecraft as it orbited the moon. The tree species were: Loblolly Pine, American Sycamore, Sweetgum, Douglas Fir and Coast Redwood. On their return to Earth, the seeds were planted and 420 of them germinated successfully. They are now planted across the United States as well as in other countries that received them as gifts. They are colloquially known as Moon Trees. Rather unsurprisingly, no other trees are known to have left the planet, orbited the moon and then returned back to Earth.

The first tree to have it's genome sequenced was the Western Balsalm Poplar in 2006.

By the time a tree has reached the age of 40 years old, it will have stored 1 ton of Carbon Dioxide in it's tissues.

There are 126 species of Pine in the world, many of which are of economic importance for their timber. Only one species of the 126 is native to the Southern hemisphere, Sumatran Pine.

The growing shoots of the Limber Pine of North America are so flexible that they can be tied into knots without breaking. The Latin name of the tree reflects this, *Pinus flexilis*.

The Monterey Pine is a highly valued timber producing tree and as such, it is the most widely planted Pine in the world. However, as a naturally occurring tree, it is, sadly, one of the rarest trees in the world and is listed as endangered by the world conservation union, the IUCN.

Mexico is home to some rare and only recently discovered conifers. The Martinez Spruce, growing in the north of the country and nowhere else in the world, was only discovered in 1981. Also only found in the north of Mexico is the Chihuahua Spruce, which was discovered in 1942. With a name like that it is no surprise it was overlooked for so long...

You may be surprised to learn that Brazil's chief timber export is not from a tropical hardwood, it is actually from a conifer, the Parana Pine. The tree's name is misleading, the tree isn't a Pine at all, it belongs to the *Araucaria* genus and is in fact very closely related to the Monkey Puzzle, which is itself often confusingly called the Chilean Pine...

Fuschia plants are a real garden staple in Britain, the small shrubs being extremely popular and widely used in borders throughout the country. What many of the gardeners who plant them don't realise is that another member of the Fuschia family is a proper tree, growing to up to 15m in height in its native New Zealand.

If you think Stinging Nettles are a pain when out and about in the countryside, then it is probably best that you don't go to Australia. In the tropical forests in the east of the country, there is the related, but altogether much bigger, Stinging Tree. It can reach 40m (over 130ft) in height and like its smaller cousin, the leaves are covered with stinging hairs. Unlike their smaller cousins though, stings from the Stinging Tree result in a severe reaction that is extremely painful and can last for many months. It is not known if there are tree versions of Dock leaves growing there...

The rather strangely named Bastard Cabbage is actually a tree that can reach 35m (115ft) in height. The bark has long been used by native tribes of the Central American region in which it grows as a worming medicine, a laxative and as a narcotic!

It was believed that the Tambalacoque Tree of Mauritius was in danger of following its fellow Mauritian species, the Dodo, to extinction. The tree produces large seeds that are covered with a thick husk and it was believed that to germinate, the seed had had to have been broken into by the large heavy bill of the Dodo. Without the Dodo, the seeds could no longer germinate. This theory was backed up by the fact that the only remaining trees were hundreds of years old with no younger ones to be found. Recently however, it has been discovered that the ground mammals introduced by man (that were the primary cause of the Dodo's extinction) have also been eating the seeds and seedlings of the Tambalacoque. Once these mammals were fenced out of areas, the tree reappeared. Sadly the Dodo is long gone.

There is an old Apple Tree growing in the grounds of Woolsthorpe Manor in Lincolnshire, England that, apart from it's age, doesn't really appear to be any different to the many other Apple Trees that are growing in the surrounding area. There is one difference though that has made this tree a bit of a visitor attraction. Isaac Newton once lived at Woolsthorpe and it was there that he formulated his theory of gravity after supposedly watching an apple fall from the tree.

Old 78rpm phonograph records were made from a substance called Shellac, a resin produced by the Lac Bug of India. The insect produces the resin as a waste product whilst feeding on the sap of the Indian Jujube Tree. Plantations of Jujube trees were deliberately grown for the Lac Bugs to feed on them so that the Shellac could be harvested. From tree sap to insect wee to music, that really is taking the ...

If it had been released many decades earlier The Joshua Tree album by the Irish band U2 could well of been made from an insects wee. Joshua Trees are members of the Yucca family, the actual tree that featured on the front cover of the album grew in the Mojave desert in America and became a must see for U2 fans from all over the globe. Unfortunately in the year 2000, it died and fell over, nowadays the site of the tree is marked with a small plaque to commemorate it. The album sold over 25 million copies and is one of the best selling albums of all time.

The forked branches of the American tree the Witch-Hazel are believed to be the best for divining for underground water.

Every state of the United States has an official tree, but the country doesn't have an official national tree.

The majority of the Grand National jumps at Aintree racecourse near Liverpool in England, are made from the branches of Spruce trees.

A Pteleologist is someone that studies the complex taxonomy of Elm trees.

The Royal Oak is the third commonest pub name in Britain, with over 600 pubs using it as their name.

One study concluded that Oak trees are more likely to be struck by lightning than any other species of tree of the same height. Shocking.

Sumac wood glows under UV light; presumably the tree looks great in a nightclub.

The world's most famous painting, the Mona Lisa by Leonardo da Vinci, is painted directly on to a board of Poplar wood.

Teak trees are large trees from the tropics producing quality timber, they belong to the Mint family, don't muddle them up when making mojitos!

The Sausage Tree of tropical Africa is very well named. The fruits of the tree do indeed look just like sausages and even hang down on stalks making them resemble the chorizo and salami you may see in a delicatessens.

The timber from Palm trees is very different from the timber of other trees. For a start it doesn't produce annual growth rings.

The most popular tree for the art of Bonsai in the world is the Chinese Elm. Despite this popularity among mini tree enthusiasts, it can potentially grow to 18m (just under 60ft) in height.

New Caledonia is a large island in the Pacific Ocean that is full of endemic trees. One of them, *Pycnandra acuminata*, has evolved to deal with the heavily polluted volcanic soil that can be found in parts of the island by accumulating the heavy metals present in the soil into its timber. When dried, over a quarter of the wood's weight is made up of Nickel.

Silk Moth caterpillars feed on the leaves of the White Mulberry tree before they then weave their silky cocoons in which they pupate and transform into an adult moth. We humans have long exploited the silk from these cocoons, it is estimated that about 4,000 White Mulberry leaves have to be consumed by caterpillars so that we can produce just one silk blouse.

The Blue Jacaranda Tree is a popular ornamental species in many parts of the world. It is rightly highly valued for the abundant blue flowers it produces every spring. Pretoria in South Africa is widely known as Jacaranda City due to the vast number of the trees that are planted all around it; every spring the tree turns this urban environment blue.

For lovers of the board game Monopoly it will come as no surprise that the most expensive tree in Britain is found in Mayfair, London. Situated in Berkeley Square, the London Plane tree has been valued by the local authority as being worth £750,000. It is not known how much it would cost to build a hotel on it!

The Common Yew, like several trees, is dioecious, meaning that they are either male or female (other trees, called monoecious, have both male and female reproductive organs). There are two Common Yew trees in Northern Ireland known as the Crom Yews; one is male, the other is female, the trees have grown entwined together, supposedly making them the most romantic trees in Great Britain according to a recent survey.

The Bialbero de Casorzo in Piedmont, Italy has to be one of the most unique trees in the world. It is actually two trees, one growing on top of the other. The lower tree is a Mulberry Tree, which has been pollarded many times, this pollarding has resulted in the tree having a rather flat top to its main trunk. From this flat topped trunk a Wild Cherry grows straight up and is now twice the height of the tree it stands on.

It is illegal to sell, distribute or propagate the following trees in New Zealand: Tree of Heaven; Japanese Spindle; Queensland Poplar; Japanese Walnut; Tree Privet; Fire Tree; Lodgepole Pine; Black Cherry; Grey Willow and Crack Willow. You have been warned!

And finally, to end. The Monkey Puzzle is one of the most well known trees in Britain with its distinct shape and foliage. It belongs to the genus *Araucaria*, species from this genus dominated the landscape of the Jurassic period (200 million years ago) when many of the largest dinosaurs were roaming the Earth. It is believed that the huge long necked sauropod dinosaurs of that era evolved their long necks to browse the leaves of these typically very tall trees. The spiky branches typical of the Monkey Puzzle have nothing at all to do with puzzling monkeys; they are there to protect the tree from dinosaurs.

www.ingramcontent.com/pod-product-compliance
Lightning Source LLC
Chambersburg PA
CBHW060159290526
45789CB00003B/1083